Building Community:

Rural Voices for Hope and Change:

An Oregon Perspective

Neal C. Lemery, J.D.

NEAL C. LEMERY

Copyright © 2020 Neal C. Lemery

All rights reserved.

ISBN: 978-1-659-924209-6

Other Books by Neal C. Lemery

Mentoring Boys to Men: Climbing Their Own Mountains (2015)

Homegrown Tomatoes: Essays and Musings from My Garden (2016)

Finding My Muse on Main Street (2018) a novel

Building Community: Rural Voices for Hope and Change: An Oregon Perspective

Published by Happy House Press, Tillamook, Oregon 97141, USA

The names of some individuals in these stories has been changed and their identifying characteristics have been changed, and some factual details have been fictionalized to protect their privacy and identify. Quotes from named persons are based on my notes, recollections, and transcriptions.

Library of Congress cataloging-in-publication data:

Lemery, Neal C.

Building Community: Rural Voices for Hope and Change: An Oregon Perspective – 1st ed.

Summary: Building community is the work of everyone. In rural communities, there are diverse talents and work in progress to improve community services, relationships, and to further collective societal values and organizations. Active community involvement engages everyone, to address social conditions and improve our collective lives. In part, this book gives voice to diverse points of views and experiences and shows the strengths and talents of rural Oregon communities.

    1.   English language --- Communities, social action. 2. Non-fiction – essays. 3. Social science ---collective activism.
ISBN: 978-1-65924209-6

Library of Congress No.

Printed in the United States of America

First Edition

DEDICATION

To my wife, Karen Keltz, for her encouragement, direction and wisdom, and all who strive to improve our communities.

A special appreciation to all those friends and neighbors who shared those "brief moments" of conversations. I heard so many inspiring snippets of life, the joys, the sorrows, the "ordinarinesss" of life that is so rich and meaningful, and which inspired this book. You generously shared stories and honest observations of your rich and productive lives, and I honor you for being decent, good citizens .

NEAL C. LEMERY

NEAL C. LEMERY

NEAL C. LEMERY

ACKNOWLEDGMENTS

I am very grateful for all of the contributors to this book, those who have submitted their observations and comments, those who have offered ideas and insights, and for all the people who I have met who are improving their communities

NEAL C. LEMERY

Introduction

Building community is a life-long task, and an all-consuming obligation of humans Every generation has been engaged in various aspects of building a community. From the savannas of the African plains to the pathways leading to every corner of the Earth, individuals have always been a part of community.

"Community" has many meanings, from the bond between mother and child, to family, to larger social units such as clans, tribes, villages, cities, and nations. Today, many people identify community to include continents, even the entire world.

Community encompasses our best and our worst expressions of our humanity, and our individual and collective wisdom on how we live our lives and find our fundamental purposes. It encompasses the fruits of our labors and is an expression of our desire to leave our descendants with the benefit of what we have created.

Community is both our birthright and our legacy. Who we are comes from our community and how we live our lives shapes and transforms where and how we live into what we desire for ourselves and the ones we love.

Community is defined by all of our best talents and efforts, and our deepest fears and crises. Like the proverbial stone thrown in a pond, our actions and our beliefs rile up the waters of our community pond, changing the lives of our neighbors and reshaping the social environment of our civilization. We are instruments of change and reformation, and what is "community" is a product of our biggest dreams and our most difficult challenges.

This book takes us on a journey through a community, the north Oregon Coast. This examines our strengths and weaknesses; gives us insight on who we are, where we've been and where we are going.

In this community, relationships are usually long term and multi-generational. I'm a fourth-generation citizen here; my roots and the roots of this community run deep and are often very interwoven and complicated. Many of us live close to the land and the sea, and the number of cows tended to by the dairy industry outnumbers people. 92% of our county is forested, and we are often buffeted by the winds and currents of the Pacific Ocean.

These are the stories of many of my friends and neighbors, their accumulated wisdom and experiences. We intermarry, and our lives are continually in contact with each other, a community which is formed by even smaller communities. Our tightness with each other is both a benefit and a detriment to how we see ourselves and how we live our lives. We don't live anonymously or isolated.

We have connection, value and expectations with each other.

In crisis, we tap into our great strength to be involved and compassionate. Our core values come into play. We gather around the community "campfire" and help one another. While modern fads and trends swirl around us, and we, like other Americans, often feel caught up in the whirlwinds and tumult of Twenty-first Century American life, we also live and celebrate our decency and our basic human aspirations.

In these times, these stories need to be told. They need to be heard and serve as models for good living, for healthy communities; serving as a call to action to live healthy lives, in service to each other and humanity.

1 ---TROY – TRADITIONAL ENGAGEMENT IN A NON-TRADITIONAL WORLD

"If you want to build a ship, don't drum up people to collect wood and don't assign them tasks and work, but rather teach them to long for the endless immensity of the sea."

---Antoine de Saint-Exupery, *The Little Prince*

Troy Downing is an Oregon State University Extension Agent, specializing in dairy productivity, manure management, and nutrient cycling. His duties take him all over the state, and he supervises other agents dealing with a wide range of agricultural issues. A father, teacher, scientist and community member, Troy manages the local extension office and has served on the local school board. He grew up in rural California and brings a wide range of experience and perspective to his community.

How do we enhance and build our community? We pay attention to our youth, which is our future.

What matters most is motivating them to be curious, and to drive that curiosity in a wide variety of activities.

When you compare Chinese youth and American youth, the Chinese kids excel at their specialty, such as math or science. American kids are less skilled at specific work but are more curious about the world and inter-relationships. As problem solvers,

American kids see more of the big picture, and can better think outside of the box.

This skill set comes from a broad-based education, and exposure to a wide variety of disciplines and approaches to problems.

While we live in an Age of Information, all of the technology and all of the data readily accessible actually stifles creativity and awareness.

The 4-H model works and has been historically successful in developing curiosity in kids, because it is "project learning", taking on a problem that is multi-layered, complex, and "cuts across" the various academic disciplines, and requires ingenuity, initiative, and curiosity.

Of equal, if not greater value, is that 4-H programs partner curious kids with engaging adults, working together informally, outside of the formal classroom, and working on a project together. This interaction, this partnership of a concerned, caring adult who works as a mentor and tutor, as well as a role model, establishes a multi-generational bond. The relationship models curious adulthood and gives youth a model for lifelong learning and lifelong success in solving a complex problem.

The most important gift to a child is a parent's time, time when they are engaged with each other, and the parent, or the helpful adult, can interact with the child, and demonstrate them the values of healthy curiosity and complex problem solving.

A 4-H club that focuses on raising livestock is really not about raising livestock, but about cultivating and enhancing multi-generational relationships, fostering curiosity, and demonstrating the value of multi-disciplinary thinking and problem solving. The livestock are some of the tools, but the real work is done in strengthening relationships and showing the power of the curious mind.

In doing that work and that learning together, the youth and the adult both are builders of community. They feel valued, they are engaged, and they become givers.

It is in giving that we realize the fruits of community life, and the values that we have in our lives, and our lifetime purpose. Giving builds confidence.

By setting high standards and a high bar for success in working on a project together, youth become engaged and challenged. They grow and learn that hard work and a focus on complex problem solving has its special rewards, including self-esteem and self-confidence. One's curiosity is the fuel to engage them in the work and their maturity into responsible adults.

In our educational system, kids enter kindergarten curious, energetic and passionate about learning. Too often, by the time they leave high school, they dread school, they struggle, and leave with a lack of enthusiasm for learning, and not able to ask questions about the world, and the problems they are challenged to solve. We need to ask ourselves why that happens, why we have a 50% high school dropout rate, why so many students don't go on to learn skills for meaningful careers, whether that be a trade or an academic program.

Relying on standardized tests to measure success, and the resulting low test scores really doesn't measure the fostering of curiosity and effective problem solving. Poor test results are shown to kids as evidence of their failure, when we should be boosting their self-esteem, improving their realistic and effective problem solving, and engaging them with adults in their lives with whom they establish positive and integrative work models.

Instead, we stifle kids, pigeon-holing them by how they take standardized tests, and fail to challenge them with complex problems where they can utilize and sharpen their problem solving skills and their innate ability to see the big picture, and apply a variety of skills in finding patterns, developing hypotheses and being able to work with others on finding solutions.

We need to get kids outdoors, where nature provides stimulation and challenges. Kids, like the rest of society, are spending too much time on their electronic screens, and are losing the art of conversation and interaction, and the social skills that come with just being with others, talking and sharing a love for life, and, being curious. What works is to engage our youth in non-traditional programs, which promote the value of education, entrepreneurialism, and small businesses.

The community has other viable organizations, which build community is other ways. Faith in Action, a program of the Tillamook Regional Medical Facility, has an innovative approach.

"Faith in Action provides hearts and hands that assist people of all ages to enrich lives with hope and joy.

"Faith in Action offers assistance and support to the frail and elderly and people of all ages who suffer from chronic illness, mental illness or disabilities through in-home volunteer services and through Wellspring, an adult respite day care center." https://www.adventisthealth.org/tillamook/about-us/volunteer/faith-in-action/

Volunteers perform yard work, provide transportation, and visiting, which engages other community members and provides much needed socialization. The Wellspring day respite program, sited in local churches, gives relief to caregivers and a social setting and meals for people who are house-bound and need continual care.

"This is a model to replicate," Troy says, highlighting the cross-generational engagement and social interaction. "It is, literally, faith in action."

The Elks Lodges, one of the nation's largest fraternal organizations, was very active during the Great Depression, acting as a local coordinator of basic services, and being a center of community response in times of almost universal need. We should return to that model of community caretaking and grass-roots organization to crises.

The fundamental questions we should ask ourselves are:

- What do students really need?

- How can we foster learning marketable skills?

- How can we offer access to higher education, in times when the costs of college are sky-high, and the rate of increases in tuition and other costs far outstrip inflation? Prior generations enjoyed wide access to higher education, and financial barriers were surmountable, regardless of one's class or economic status. Public universities are the great social levelers and the stairway to improving one's skills; the big promoters of life-long learning.

- How can we engage more students and foster the level of curiosity and desire for self-improvement, while making college affordable? We are moving into an era where a four-year degree is most easily attainable through community colleges and transfer degrees. On-line and distance learning technology can bring excellent teachers and the collegiate classroom experience of discussion and diverse viewpoints to rural areas.

As a school board member, Troy was encouraged to visit the schools and see what is really going on in education. As a parent, he was focused on what was good for his kids. As a school board member, the challenge was to look at what is good for everyone's kids. Are we offering what kids need?

The challenge was to be the observer and take in what teachers were doing and what kids were learning. The diversity of kids and the wide range of learning issues in the school were challenging, yet teachers had the skills and patience to reach kids and provide educational opportunities that Troy felt he would be unable to provide if that kid was his own child. The challenges today in education are daunting, yet attainable.

Diversity stimulates curiosity. Exposure to diversity promotes creativity. This is truer now in this Information Age. We don't need to be the best, but we need to be good at engaging kids in a diverse, challenging environment, where their natural curiosity is honored, where they team up with adult role models in a community learning environment, such as a 4-H program after school.

This diversity is much broader than cultural or racial. We need diverse learning situations and a wide range of people with different learning styles, different experiences, and different views of the world. Together, curious kids who aren't afraid to learn can be coached to develop solutions to a wide range of problems.

When kids are matched with adults who care about them, and care about the development of their minds, they experience how the adult approaches a situation, and they learn wider problem-solving skills. They learn confidence and develop the mental muscle to be effective learners and responsible adults.

Foreign exchange students told the school board after their year of living in the community and experiencing an American high school that their own country's classes were more challenging and demanding more of their intellectual skills. Yet, the American high school made them feel special, unique, that they were truly their own person. They felt valued as an individual.

A well-rounded curriculum develops self-worth and rewards one's own passions and curiosity. Life-long curiosity and question asking skills become developed, and empowered students become life-long learners and effective community members.

2 ---- STACIE – COMING BACK AND BUILDING US UP

"Community is not an ideal; it is people. It is you and me. In community we are called to love people just as they are with their wounds and their gifts, not as we want them to be." —Jean Vanier, *From Brokenness to Community*

Stacie Zuercher is a people person, who came back to her hometown to make it an even better place for everyone. Down to earth, practical, sharp witted, and having a contagious laugh that warms your heart. She uses both her passion and her humor in challenging situations, bringing the group back to the main issues and unifying everyone with the common goals.

Stacie serves the community and the State of Oregon as the Community Programs Supervisor, Northwest Senior and Disability Services, which serves Tillamook County.

"My goal is to assess the need, implement and provide oversight to programs that promote health and wellness within the community including inner-agency programs, planning and facilitating healthcare initiatives and providing oversight to Older American Act Programs serving vulnerable seniors and people with disabilities.," Stacie says.

What is a fundamental strength (building block) in your community? Why does your community have this particular strength?

"I believe that we have very strong leadership that has a vision for what this community could look like if agencies, local businesses, community partners and stewards in our community were focused not only on individual goals but that we are all working towards fostering a healthy community. For example, Bill Baertlein and the (other) county commissioners declared 2015 the "Year of Wellness in our community" which led to the fight against diabetes and making efforts to lower the number of people who have a diagnosis of diabetes. There was already amazing collaboration in our community but things like this assisted in people deepening their relationships, networks, and support to one another. I've said many times that the soil was rich for this growth, it was the right time."

What is a significant contribution you have made to community building? Why did you do this?

"I have been very engaged in Tillamook County Wellness since it started four years ago. I have served as a Task Force member, was a lead in the Community Outreach committee, am a current member of the Access to Healthy Foods committee and go to Committee Chair leadership meetings to provide support and insight. I have also done event planning to create various health opportunities for community members (at no cost to the consumer), such conferences, activities and lectures."

What talents and resources did you use?

"I have planned and facilitated hundreds of events throughout my professional career and can organize, present and leads events with ease. My attitude and enthusiasm they say, is also a strength. I usually bring to the table a, 'I'll bring the coffee, you bring the snacks, let's buckle down and get it done' kind of a mindset. Additionally, I have well developed relationships with many community members and leaders which assists in collaborative efforts and problem solving. I also represent a vulnerable population and have great passion for being a voice for seniors and people with disabilities."

What does your community do well? Why? What do people contribute to move this work ahead?

"I am consistently impressed with the level of commitment that people have in this community. The agency leaders I work with are so passionate, hardworking and committed to providing support and services that contributes to changing the culture in regard to how we perceive health in our community. It's really amazing to get the privilege of being a part of it. Additionally, I love that it is a priority to bring more opportunities to people so they can easily make healthy choices. For example; creating more clean and safe trails for walking really encourages people to exercise."

What is your role in community building? How do people view your role?

"My role is to participate in the agency partnerships and provide resources and support to people who would otherwise slip through the cracks. My background is in Social Work, so it has been an incredible opportunity to have a part in the success of bringing those skills to the Public Health charge and assist in bringing more exciting opportunities to the masses. I'm incredibly proud to participate in programs that are successful and love it when I hear that other communities are studying the work that has been done in Tillamook County so they can replicate it in their own communities. That is the definition of success for me."

"I believe that people view my role as important because as I said, I represent a specific population that is at times underserved."

Could you give me a one paragraph resume'?

Stacie Zuercher

Community Programs Supervisor

Northwest Senior and Disability Services, serving Tillamook County.

My goal is to assess the need, implement and provide oversight to programs that promote health and wellness within the community including inner-agency programs, planning and facilitating healthcare initiatives and providing oversight to Older American Act Programs serving vulnerable seniors and people with disabilities.

Bachelor of Science Degree, Social Science

Portland State University

Portland, OR

Masters Certificate, Gerontology

Pacific University

Forest Grove, OR

"In our community, and I suspect in all communities, the underserved, the poor, the elderly, tend to be invisible to much of the rest of the community. They are not usually the movers and shakers, the leaders of organizations. They have worked hard and raised families and been a big part of the community their entire lives.

"Or they have moved here to retire, attracted by our rural character, the natural beauty, perhaps to be closer to family and friends.

"Few institutions and organizations focus on the elderly population. There are senior centers and meal sites. Yet, these facilities struggle financially, and the needs far exceed available resources. Churches are facing an aging and declining population of parishioners, and transportation and housing are significant barriers to living in our area.

"We now have a public bus system, yet those resources are spread thin due to our large geographical area and financial resources. The "dial a ride" program allows seniors to make their doctor appointments and meet other needs, yet that service is also limited by financial constraints and the availability of vans.

"Seniors often don't have the financial resources to maintain their homes or make modifications so that they can remain in their homes. Most homes have steps or stairways, and someone who has broken a limb or must rely on a walker or wheelchair finds that physical barriers can prevent them from remaining in their home. The upheaval to their lives in relocating, and the financial costs to society are tremendous, and often shorten people's lifespans and deteriorate their quality of life."

Stacie has been the local champion of the "Ramps and Rails" program. She has partnered with the local chapter of Habitat for Humanity and has assembled a team of local service clubs, contractors, and other volunteers.

Not only are wheelchair ramps available, but handrails on steps and ramps. Grip bars for showers and other risky areas around the house are also easily installed. The coordinator has some generic plans, local merchants often donate materials, and contractors often volunteer their time. Most projects are completed within a day. ∫

And, voila, a dangerous situation for a person is now much safer. The home becomes much more habitable. Sometimes, the work is needed before the person can come home from the hospital or a rehab center. This work is often the deciding factor on whether or not a person can stay in their home or have to look at an assisted care facility, at a much greater cost.

Stacie coordinates other services, too, keeping in touch with local food banks, meals on wheels, churches and other organizations. A lot of this work isn't formal and bureaucratic. In a small community, everyone knows all the players, and relationships are nurtured over phone calls, coffee, and numerous meetings and events. This is networking on steroids, rich and vibrant, continually re-energized by success stories and numerous community events.

One of the programs that Stacie has nurtured and supported is Wellspring. This program is hosted by a local church, offering a "day care" for people needing extensive care. The caregivers get a much-needed break and the recipients are around other recipients and caregivers. They get a meal, some individual attention and some much-needed social interaction outside of their homes. There are a few activities and it is a productive day "out of the house".

Once a month, Stacie meets with other social service professionals in the community. They see each other in meetings and interact on a case by case basis as needed. But their monthly meeting is a time to get together, without the urgent demands of a particularly challenging case, and look at the bigger picture.

Each group member can share some insight, a trend, news about a new or developing program. Brainstorming is rampant and contagious, and relationships are strengthened, both professionally and personally. Problems and snags in the system are identified, discussed, and subject to some intense problem solving, and everyone is brought up to date on urgent and compelling issues.

Stacie is in the middle of all that energy and all that relationship building and strengthening. Her intimate knowledge of the community, and the players in the "system", are invaluable. She works her magic, offering inspiration and wise counsel, and works towards solutions.

Her many statewide and national contacts and relationships come into play, and she's able to gather facts and network strategies, and bring that back to the group, again weaving and strengthening the social services web in the community.

The monthly gathering is also self-care and professional support for the members. Being a professional in a small community is, by its nature, isolating and solitary. You are often the "only one" who is doing a particular job and has a particular expertise and knowledge base. The problems on your desk are seemingly unique and often daunting. Who do you have to process with, to brainstorm a solution?

Stacie cuts across all those isolating factors, often with her cheery "can do" attitude and sense of humor and determination. She is fierce and focused when it comes to getting to the heart of a problem, not easily believing that there is nothing that can be done.

In all this, she is seen as a tremendous resource, a person who has been around the block. The current urgent issue is not her first rodeo, and she's able to think out loud, develop a dialogue, and come up with some strategies. And, if nothing great comes to mind, she'll know who she can connect with who will likely have that brilliant idea or the missing piece of the puzzle.

Great leadership in government is not always restricted to the centers of power and the big cities. Brilliant ideas, workable solutions, and healthy, vibrant relationships are often found in the small towns and communities, where people like Stacie are working their magic, weaving their relationships, and capitalizing on the strengths of the rest of the community.

3 --- PAUL – THE EDUCATOR

One of the driving forces and strength builders in our community is Paul Erlebach. He's the superintendent of Neah-Kah-Nie School District, a small district in north Tillamook County, Oregon. In a small community, the schools are part of the heart of the community. Schools change lives and offer hope for youth for the future. The district motto is "Preparing Children for an Everchanging World".

"As the Neah-Kah-Nie Superintendent, Paul strives to ensure all students have access to the highest quality education and collaboratively works with teachers, classified staff, district office staff, school principals, the Neah-Kah-Nie School District Board of Directors, volunteers, and community members to honor this commitment.

Paul values the community support given to Neah-Kah-Nie students and encourages parents and community members to make a difference in the lives of youth by mentoring or volunteering." http://nknsd.org.

The schools have a challenging task. In a rural area, students face daunting challenges, including poverty, hunger, access to medical care, affordable housing and transportation.   Over half of the kids qualify for subsidized school meals, and family wage jobs are scarce.

Yet, there is a sense of unity and purpose in the schools, with a dedicated staff, many of whom being long term residents and graduates of local schools.   There is strong community support, and avid community participation in athletics and academic activities. Local foundations contribute funds and expertise to cultivate and enrich school programs, and local professionals and experts are often in the schools teaching and mentoring. There is a local culture of advocacy for public schools and providing meaningful and challenging opportunities for all students.

90% of parents attend parent-teacher conferences. Extensive capital improvements have been made, supported by a $16 million-dollar capital improvement bond approved by the voters and state money. All elementary students have access to swimming lessons.

The schools are small, and the staff is collegial and supportive. Being innovative is encouraged. The high school principal and a teacher were recently recognized as top in their field by Oregon educators.

What is a fundamental strength (building block) in your community?

"A fundamental strength in the six communities (Bay City, Garibaldi, Rockaway Beach, Wheeler, Nehalem, Manzanita) that comprise the Neah-Kah-Nie School District is the support. Community members whole heartedly support youth, their activities, education, and future. Community partners who support youth include parents, Mudd Nick Foundation, business owners, Eugene Schmuck Foundation, Neah-Kah-Nie Youth Athletics, Rockaway

Beach Lions Club, Neah-Kah-Nie Education Foundation, Ann Parks Fund, Rinehart Clinic, and many others."

Why does your community have this particular strength?

"I believe the community has this particular strength because youth are a vital part of each community. Neah-Kah-Nie School District is fortunate to retain the "small school feel" at each school. Each school is a "community school." Community members are immensely proud of this fact. Patrons have local control of the school district and local finances; this is rare in Oregon."

What is a significant contribution you have made to community building?

"As the Neah-Kah-Nie School District Superintendent, my most significant contribution is the advocacy I have for youth. Sometimes I am the only voice youth have at the table, this is an important contribution. I am active in Rockaway Beach Lions Club, Rinehart Clinic, and Mudd Nick Foundation."

Why did you do this?

"Youth are my clients, the people I serve."

What talents and resources did you use?

"I am an attentive listener, quiet leader, Spanish speaker, active learner, visible in the community, and goal oriented."

What does your community do well?

"Prioritize youth and include youth in decision making."

Why?

"A mutual dependency. Through the example of youth, older people have an appreciation for new experiences. Older people mentor youth for satisfaction; not obligation."

What do people contribute to move this work ahead?

"People contribute in a variety of ways, through positive parenting, active board & club membership, coaching, mentoring, and contributing."

What is your role in community building?

"I try to be a catalyst, comforter, supporter, and giver."

How do people view your role?

"People appreciate that I am visible in the community and contribute to the welfare of its citizens."

Could you give me a one paragraph resume'?

"I was born and raised in Eastern Oregon.

BA Southern Oregon State University, BA Eastern Oregon University, MA Portland State, Administrator License, Lewis & Clark College

Spanish teacher/English as a Second Language Coordinator-11 years

Elementary and Middle School Principal-12 years

Neah-Kah-Nie School District Superintendent-8 years

Married to Rosa Maria Zavala de Erlebach, daughter Gracia and son Paul Daniel."

Why is Paul an effective leader in the community? He's out and about, in the schools, at community events, and active in several service organizations. Everyone knows Paul. He's approachable, engaging, and also eager to share his passion for kids and for education. He works behind the scenes, informing, listening, and building coalitions for programs and activities that will help kids.

He is respected and engages with the Hispanic population. Being bilingual and married to a native Spanish speaker gives him access and credibility. He models cultural diversity and inclusiveness, in his quiet and effective way.

4 --- MIS ---- TAKING ON FOOD SCARCITY

The person in our community who is the focal point, the leader of efforts to take on this issue is Melissa "Mis" Swanson-Carlson. She's the local director of the Oregon Food Bank. She's often "behind the scenes" but a mover and shaker, and the "go to person" when it comes to issues of poverty, scarcity, and social concerns.

She's one of those "connectors" in a community, continually putting people in touch with each other, a walking Rolodex of contacts and resources, and the person who truly lives Robert Kennedy's quote: "Some men see things as they are and ask why. I dream of things that never were, and ask why not."

Food scarcity is a major issue in rural America.

"In 2018, an estimated one in nine Americans were food insecure, equating to over 37 million Americans, including more than 11 million children.

"The U.S. Department of Agriculture (USDA) defines food insecurity as a lack of consistent access to enough food for an active, healthy life. It is important to know that though hunger and food insecurity are closely related, they are distinct concepts. Hunger refers to a personal, physical sensation of discomfort, while food insecurity refers to a lack of available financial resources for food at the household level.

"Extensive research reveals food insecurity is a complex problem. Many people do not have the resources to meet their basic needs, challenges which increase a family's risk of food insecurity. Though food insecurity is closely related to poverty, not all people living below the poverty line experience food insecurity and people living above the poverty line can experience food insecurity.

"Food insecurity does not exist in isolation, as low-income families are affected by multiple, overlapping issues like lack of affordable housing, social isolation, chronic or acute health problems, high medical costs, and low wages. Taken together, these issues are important social determinants of health, defined as the "conditions in the environments in which people are born, live, learn, work, play, worship and age that affect a wide range of health, functioning and quality-of-life outcomes and risks." Effective responses to food insecurity must address the overlapping challenges posed by the social determinants of health. Hunger + Health explores the impact of food insecurity as a social determinant of health and its effect on individual and population health outcomes. —understand-food-insecurity. (Feeding America.org)

Food insecurity is invisible, yet about 60% of our school kids qualify for free and reduced school breakfast and lunch. Slightly less than a third of local residents receive "food stamps" (SNAP benefits), and about 10,000 out of our 25,000 residents live below the federal poverty level.

During the last recession, about 40% of county residents accessed local food banks and food pantries.

Access to food has expanded. There are now food pantries in every community, all the high schools and the community college. The library distributes seed packets every spring (about three seed packets per county resident), and the Seeds to Supper program teaches sustainable home gardening principles. Some communities have community gardens, and there are free evening supper programs throughout the community.

Home gardeners and the local master gardeners program frequently deliver produce to the food pantries and food banks, and bins are available at all the grocery stores so that people can donate canned goods.

A local restaurant puts on a community Thanksgiving dinner, by donation, with all the proceeds donated to the food bank. No one is turned away.

What is a fundamental strength (building block) in your community? Tillamook County has a strong culture of collaboration and peer mentoring amongst its' Social Service and Non-Profit agencies.

Why does your community have this particular strength?

"I believe that this collaborative spirit was formed began before my time in the county, with a big part being a FEAST event that was held in Tillamook County over 12 years ago or so, which brought many agencies, governmental, non-profit, for-profit, etc. together to discuss our community(ies), what was going well, what needed attention, and lead to action teams to address certain areas. That is where the Social Directors Network was born. Another reason is that Ford Family Foundation invested in our county with the Ford Family Foundation Leadership Cohorts, identifying and building leadership within our community. This started about the same time and extended into 2014. Many other similar models have come and invested further into our community in similar and specific ways, which continued to grow our broad culture of collaboration."

What is a significant contribution you have made to community building?

"Working collaboratively with Erin Skaar, CARE, Inc., and Tillamook County Commissioner, Bill Baertlein, identifying the Housing Crisis in Tillamook County, raising awareness, and moving quickly to developing a community approach to developing solutions that are sustainable, effective, and impactful. This started with the Community Vitality Project, which lead to formation of the TC Housing Task Force, and ultimately the formation of the Tillamook County Housing Commission."

Why did you do this?

"I feel very strongly about working collaboratively with community partners to work toward and maintain a vital community. Housing is a basic need that is not being met for so many in our community, from individuals who are experiencing extreme poverty, to working families who are impacted by the lack of housing inventory available to families and individuals who cannot access the inventory that is available at or above $300,000."

What talents and resources did you use?

"I care very deeply about people and community, so relationship building and connecting are core to who I am and how I navigate in the world. I am blessed to have an employer that allows me and expects me to contribute to a strong community and community development, which gives me the bandwidth, resources, and encouragement to utilize my strengths. Addressing root causes of issues works is essential to developing long term, sustainable solutions."

What does your community do well? Why?

"Our community loves well. We come together to celebrate each other, our environment, our traditions. We mourn together, we support each other in times of need and strive to improve how we care for one another. We know that many needs are not being met and it drives us to continue to work collaboratively to try to improve incrementally, because we care."

What do people contribute to move this?

"People in our community contribute time, money, materials, ideas, vision, planning, and passion to all the work in our community."

What is your role in community building?

"I'm a mentor, connector, leader, supporter, problem solver, mediator, doer, facilitator, peer mentor, volunteer, and sounding board."

How do people view your role?

"Supporter and connector."

Could you give me a one paragraph resume'?

"Branch Service Manager for Oregon Food Bank Tillamook County Services (7 years), Equity Ambassador for Oregon Food Bank, Northwest Parenting Education Coordinator (5 years), Caregiver, President of Food Roots Board, Member of Tillamook County Housing Commission, Director on the Tillamook County Transportation District Board, Co-Chair of Tillamook County Wellness Access to Healthy Food Committee, Previous Secretary and Treasurer of Tillamook County United Way Board, Previous Vice President of Tillamook Farmers Market, Ford Family Foundation Graduate and Community Ambassador/Community Builder, Previous President of Tillamook Kiwanis, and Previous President of Tillamook Area Chamber of Commerce."

Melissa, whom everyone refers to as "Mis", is a community builder. She's friendly, compassionate, and resourceful. She's always upping her game, too, continually keeping up on issues surrounding social services, nutrition and the many needs of those in need.

She's one of the leaders in the local monthly gathering of social service workers, who gather to collaborate, network, and brainstorm, being on the cutting edge of trends and needs, matching resources and needs. And, if there is a need for a voice, an advocate, for an urgent issue surrounding food scarcity, she is there, passionate, articulate, and positive.

She stays out of the limelight. "It's not about me," she frequently says.

But, she's one of the compassionate people in the community who quietly, consistently makes a difference in the lives of thousands of people.

5 --- NICK – THE KIDS' COP

Nick Troxel is a keystone in our community. He works in several worlds and is a bridge between the world of law enforcement and world of teens and children. He is both the tough, take care of the problem law enforcement officer, and the sweet, tender dad and older brother for kids in a tough situation.

A small-town cop sees it all. Drugs, violence, familial dysfunction, poverty, and aimlessness. His work requires him to have his feet in both roles.

His innate ability to relate to kids, to engage in tough conversations about violence, sexual abuse, bullying, drugs, and the other community problems that occupy a police officer's shift, is remarkable. He's soft spoken, gentle, compassionate, and often seen as a teddy bear. Yet, there is the other side: focused, direct, and incredibly skilled at interviewing and questioning, thorough and laser-focused on building a criminal case and ensuring that a kid is safe and protected.

It's not "good cop, bad cop", but "down to business cop, supportive friend". People trust him and know that he will take care of business if the business needs to be done.

He comes across as casual, laid back, but nothing misses his notice, and he absorbs all that he sees. He's very often in the schools, looking like he's just hanging out, Mr. Friendly. He has a genuine love for kids. And, he's an eagle, always watching, always absorbing information. He is adept at figuring out relationships and social pressures, the dynamics of teenage community.

He's well-respected and appreciated, gaining a seat on the school board as his perspective is cherished and his knowledge of the inner workings of school life giving school staff and other board members an invaluable bank of insight and knowledge. He gets to go where no other adult gets to go in the lives of our kids.

He's active in Rotary, and never a stranger to anyone in the community. His passion for kids and their safety, their well-being, is a bright light in the town.

Here's what Nick has to say about his community:

What is a fundamental strength (building block) in your community? Why does your community have this particular strength?

"I would have to say from my experience in this community I see the people as our most important strength, resource and precious asset."

What is a significant contribution you have made to community building?

"I have worked within this community since June of 2000. My profession is service driven as is my volunteerism. I would have to say my most significant contribution would be giving back to our young people in our community. I have a passion for serving those who are most vulnerable (children & adults alike). I have fostered relationships with children to young adults by planting that seed, watering it through genuine concern and caring, and then sitting back and watching them grow into beautiful, successful contributors to our community. When one stumbles and has a set-back not to hold that against them but let them know that things will get better. This is just a speed bump in the road of life."

Why did you do this?

"I have a passion for service and working with others. I know that what I do does have an everlasting impact on others. I know that this impact is powerful and can change lives. I have had contact with individuals who were going to kill themselves and have changed their minds based on the relationships I have created with them. I didn't know this at that time but was told later by the person who was going to commit suicide they decided not to because of the conversation we had that day. "

What talents and resources did you use?

"Pretty simple in my mind. I treat others as if they were my family. I always want to make sure that I am treating people with respect and dignity no matter what the situation. In addition, I make sure I do my best to be the best communicator. When I think of communication that is through words (spoken and written) and body language and appearance to others. Building relationships with resources within your community is another key component to success. When you need something, it is nice to make a phone call or show up and have that conversation with that person. It is easier to have those conversation as you have already built that relationship with that person and there is a level of trust needed that is already developed."

What does your community do well? Why? What do people contribute to move this work ahead?

"The Tillamook community comes together and works together through mutually beneficial partnerships to work towards the goals set. We work so well together that when I brag to my colleges outside of Tillamook County, they are in awe at what we can accomplish here."

What is your role in community building? How do people view your role?

"Through my professional – paid work at the Tillamook Police Department and through my volunteer work I work on numerous projects to improve and build our community. I have never thought of how others view my role. Currently I am a Detective assigned to the Tillamook School District #9 as the School Resource Officer. I have held this position once before for four years and have always maintained a relationship with the School District.

"I am currently a Tillamook School District #9 Board Member. Rotarian and past President of our Tillamook Club. I am a founding member of the Auggie's Hope Board of Directors and past President. I am the homeless liaison for the Tillamook Police Department and serve on the Helping Hands Board of Directors.

"Through all these roles I am working on continuing to build and maintain a great community."

Could you give me a one paragraph resume'?

"Detective Nick Troxel began his law enforcement career in 1995, volunteering as a Corvallis Police Cadet. In 2000, he was hired by the Oregon State Police as a Fish and Wildlife Cadet. In 2002 He was hired part time as a Crime Prevention Specialist with the City of Corvallis Police Department and was later hired full time as a Patrol Officer at the Corvallis Police Department. Nick moved to Tillamook in 2003, where he was hired as a Tillamook City Police Officer. In Tillamook Nick has been a Field Training Officer, Taser Instructor, Training Manager, Firearms Instructor, BBP Instructor, four years as the School Resource Officer, Child Abuse Detective, Narcotics Detective, homeless liaison, Every 15 Minutes Program coordinator, and a member of the Multi-Agency Major Crimes Team. He was then promoted to Detective in 2014. He has managed the Field Training Program, been a member of the Tillamook County Multi-disciplinary Teams for children, elderly and people with disabilities, and sexual assault response team member. He also serves on the Board of Directors of the Tillamook School District, Board of Directors for Helping Hands Re-Entry, current member and past President of the Rotary Club of Tillamook, and past President, founding board member for Auggie's Hope, Member of the Oregon Fallen Badge Foundation's Line of Duty Death Response Team and a member of the Oregon Fallen Badge Foundation's Board of Directors."

6 --- ASK A BUSY PERSON

This person's comments have an edge, and some well-thought-out criticism and commentary on our social relationships and some of the key players. We live in a small town and to share these thoughts, I believe some anonymity is appropriate and invites candor. As well, anonymity can preserve the networking and interactions that are so vital to a community. Anonymity often fosters honesty.

In a small town, one of the sayings spoken at a committee meeting is "ask a busy person to get it done, and it does."

It seems the busiest people are the ones who are the most productive, the most organized, the most able to "pull it all together" and take a project to the next level. They work their networks, delegate tasks and get it done.

They are often frank, getting down to the "brass tacks" and don't mince words when there's a need for an honest opinion, and directness.

One of my friends is one of those "busy people", the kind of person you want on your committee, within the circle of "doers" for something you are passionate about. I was able to fit into their hectic schedule and was blessed to have one of those rare two and a half hour lunches, where all the problems were on the table, and refreshing honesty blew through the door. Such friendships are rare, and I cherish them. They are the jewels in the community's crown.

We dug into the tough questions I had sent to them earlier, intrigued with their response to my question of what doesn't work in the community. They are always upbeat, optimistic, fired up about one of the great and fresh activities in town, the stuff that is on the cutting edge, and so new and fresh it hasn't hit the local weekly paper yet.

"Well, not really," was their response to my question of how well the community works.

Even though great things happen, exciting events, economic growth, social activities that are fresh and new, and people are engaged, we are a culture that identifies as impoverished.

True that, I have to say. Historically, we've been an isolated rural area, our main industries being undercapitalized farms, and the cyclic, boom to bust fishing and timber industries. Our tourist industry has historically been seasonal, and mostly providing minimum wage service jobs. We export our bright kids to the cities and they often don't return. We're also a retirement community, and a large share of retirees struggle financially. We have a high rate of drug and alcohol abuse, which is reflected in a busy jail and a homeless population that has a high rate of undiagnosed and untreated mental illness. Food scarcity is a serious issue.

We have a history of poor transportation and communication, and old timers refer to their trips to the inland cities as "going outside".

The mindset is complex, and newcomers are labeled as such, and often are not included or welcomed, even though they may have lived here for years, often decades, have bought homes and started businesses. Yet, they are still the outsiders.

There's a Pioneer Association here, a club that defines membership by requiring you live here for forty years. There's no real function of the association, except for a quarterly potluck, and a reduced admissions price on "Pioneer Day" at the county fair and getting a pioneer ribbon to wear that day.

But that idea that you have to earn your place here by longevity and seniority as the only criteria is an undercurrent in local culture.

We like being connected to each other. "Old families" are well connected, through generations of intermarriage and working and living in the same community.

In that, we have developed trust of each other, being connected, often an interwoven, multi-layered social fabric.

There is loyalty, yet there is reluctance to accept new ideas. You may be loyal and trust someone who has a new idea, a new methodology, a new business model. You are drawn to that, to accept it and support it. Yet, at the same time, you don't trust it, you're hesitant. We are connected, yet I'm not willing to take that next step to support your new venture.

We really don't deserve nice things, you know.

After all, we are impoverished, we are isolated. If there was a Pacific Northwest slang term for "hillbilly", we'd use that. But that term is too Southern for us. We need a word for that mindset, though.

Impoverished, isolated, we are hillbillies.

Yet we live in paradise, and we say that sentence out loud. We hear it from the tourists, and many of us make our livelihoods off of tourists who want to explore our piece of paradise. The marketing we do showcases our huge inventory of natural wonders, the ocean, large bays, rivers, long unspoiled beaches, salmon fishing, bird watching, the world's largest cheese factory, the world's largest wooden structures, gourmet beer making.   The list can grow long. The State has fueled our marketing with a restructuring of a motel and short-term lodging tax, pouring millions of tax revenue dollars from tourists into a variety of ingenious and state of the art promotional efforts.

The result is more tourists, certainly more wealthy tourists, and the industry is now catering to the high end of the market. Locals are cashing in, and it's a boom time for those with houses to rent, restaurants, and guided "experiences".

All this attention and prosperity is lovely. After all, we have nice restaurants and nice facilities near some of our favorite hang outs. There's plenty of jobs, though still a shortage of family wage jobs. The increased demand for short term rentals has sent the cost of just renting a house or an apartment through the roof. We have a housing crisis, and few entrepreneurs want to invest in reasonable cost housing for workers and families, when the real money is short term rentals for the more affluent tourists.

The other side of the coin is seen too, in conversations about being "invaded", about clogged highways and no parking at our favorite beaches and fishing spots. We bemoan the crowded grocery stores and an overabundance of RVs and tour busses. People tell of "hiding out" on summer weekends, not leaving home for fear of the congestion.

This disconnect, this contraction between loyalty and exclusion plays out at every level, my friend says.

"We can be friendly, but we often are not welcoming" my friend says.

Many people who move here, mostly retirees, have done their homework, and have researched and vetted the area. They are drawn here by the scenery, the opportunity to be in nature outside of your doorstep, the small, cozy communities, and being away, but not all that far, from the good attributes of the big city.

You can get involved in community activities and groups, and newcomers are invited. Yet, after a few years, a significant number of active retirees move away, feeling they've been quietly, persistently shunned and marginalized. They'll never live here long enough to be a member of the Pioneer Association, and they also haven't been invited out for coffee with the "old timers" and invited to join the "inner circle", the people who hold the power, politically, socially, and economically.

That mindset is changing, somewhat. The local Chamber now has a "Young Professionals" group, Millennials who bring their entrepreneurial and social marketing skills to bear in this rural area. They find their economic niche and they build their social networks and marketing acumen. They fearlessly work their magic across the Internet and are citizens of the world. Their world doesn't include the "old boy" networks; their thinking and outlooks are fresh and vigorous.

"We have livability gaps," my friend says. Despite our interwoven social networks and relationships, we lack many essentials to a healthy community life.

The local paper is part of a conglomerate of other small-town papers. The editorial page has been abandoned, as has the previously fruitful and controversial news beat of courthouse politics and controversial issues. If you want publicity for your activity, you write the press release and take the submitted photo yourself. The paper exists to sell ads and make money for the corporate office, not to well serve the community by educating us on what is happening at the city council meeting, or whether a local entrepreneur is treating their employees kindly. If you really want to go in depth on a local issue, you have to look for a different source of information.

This view of local journalism is shared in the big city. I recently heard the mayor of a major city in the state refer to their daily paper's attitude as "just enough news to wrap around a tire ad."

The crackpot letter to the editor gets published, but without a sidebar on the facts or a comment from the focus of the letter writer's attack.

This inattention to local government and local issues of interest by the media has led, in part, to the lack of competition for seats on local governing bodies. City council and school board candidates run unopposed and the meetings are not covered by the paper. Midterm vacancies are filled without competition and without public input or scrutiny.

Elections often involve voting for the familiar name, without knowing more or even knowing what questions need to be asked. Many candidates emerge because they want to take on a personal issue; they have a dog in the fight. Then, they remain on the board or the council, without really being passionate about the other pressing issues on their plate. And, they aren't held accountable for that kind of thinking and approach to public service.

Those in leadership often lack the policy making and leadership skills that are called for by their positions and the issues we face.

Yet, these public agencies make major decisions on vital issues touching on our quality of life and fundamental values.

We have a shortage of mental health services and quality health care, as well as a fully engaged social service sector that takes on addiction and child health issues. Certainly, this is a national issue, but it also goes to the issue of loyalty and quality of life.

Day care remains essentially unavailable, with no care for kids under 18 months, and costly services for older kids. Hours aren't convenient for working parents, and people scramble continually to find reliable care. Grandparents and good friends are an essential component of the day care spectrum of services. Larger employers sidestep the need, and, all too often, kids don't receive the care they need.

We are lovers of competitive sports at most levels of public education in the county. High school sports are big, and new competitions and sports are being added at the junior high and even grade school level. A local supporter donated a small fortune to install artificial turf on the high school football field, yet the performing arts and literary arts programs struggle to stay afloat and to keep highly skilled teachers. Those decisions are not on the table for discussion, and don't seem to be on the community radar screen.

My friend is as actively involved as ever and remains passionate and committed. This is a great place to work and live and there is so much that one person can accomplish here, they say.

My friend's actions remain louder than their words. Yet, they are a realist and a pragmatist. And, they are moving ahead, making the community a better place for all.

7 --- LAURA – THE EDITOR

Every community needs someone who ties us together, keeps us in touch, and is the "go to" person for news, events, and, when a crisis arises, to be the connector and disseminator of vital information.

The beauticians and barbers, the bartenders, the grocery clerk, the coffee klatch, the neighborhood "over the fence" people still are good sources of news and community activities. In the day of newspapers, reporters and editors kept the community informed with the news of the day, the community calendar, and the announcements of births, weddings, and deaths.

Today, the printed word, the weekly newspaper, even the daily paper from the big city, have changed and adapted to this electronic age, and the rising costs of staff, the competition for advertising dollars. Information is almost instantly transmitted to our smart phones and tablets, with some social commentators arguing that we now are less in touch with our neighbors and communities.

Social media can make everyone the reporter, the publisher, yet our audiences are manipulated by the algorithms of the social media conglomerates.

Not everyone is "online" and accesses this torrent of information and "social connection". In our community, a fourth of our homes lack internet access entirely. Internet speeds in rural America varies, as wired and wireless connectivity is irregular.

With the wide availability of so many apps, social media outlets, and electronic distractions, not everyone receives the same news, or is part of the same electronic community. Local news and information are often lost in the barrage of our communications.

Local organizations wanting to reach out to the community have their own social media connections, and "push out" a relentless stream of information and "media", but it often gets lost in the volume of information and "posts".

The local print media is only published once a week, and their ability to have reporters in the field is sharply limited by their own financial constraints.

In this era, the local newspaper is taking on a new form, the electronic "press", available on your computer and your portable devices.

Laura Swanson is at the center of this new revolution in communications and published media. She is passionately involved in a variety of community activities, making connections, finding stories, and writing about a broad range of subjects. She cultivates her sources and receives leads on breaking stories and personal interest items.

As a "native daughter" and living most of her life in the community, she works her connections and local knowledge to bring life to her stories, to "mine" her sources and present fresh news to the community.

She's a partner in the *"Tillamook County Pioneer"*, a community media source, and our most widely read "newspaper". It is easily available online. The *Pioneer* is widely read, and has a large following in the metropolitan area, as many of our visitors and vacation homeowners want to keep up on local news. She weaves in Twitter, Instagram and Facebook, giving the *Pioneer's* "followers" on social media a published story as it breaks. She's recently added "tidbits", short video clips highlighting recent news stories.

She takes on the bigger, more compelling stories, too: homelessness, housing, hunger, mental health issues, and environmental issues. There's a letter to the editor section, obituaries, and an occasional movie review, too. You get a free community newspaper, just a click away on your computer.

The *Pioneer* is a rich and informative asset to the community, providing us with connections and a ready source of local news and trends. There's thoughtful commentary, going in depth on complex and politically "hot" issues, informing voters and ramping up conversations going on in the coffee shops and church basements.

What does Laura see in our community? What is the state of its health?

What is a fundamental strength (building block) in your community?

"Resiliency is often identified – and in fact Oregon State University did a study on resiliency and used our area; a "sense" of community. we take care of our own; well, sorta … that's another part of the story. As our community grows who are 'our own' And how do you 'join'? "

That's one thing you get when you dig into a thoughtful question with Laura: an inquisitive, sharp mind that is always asking "why" and "what if".

Why does your community have this particular strength?

"Location; environment – living on "the edge", again it is influenced by having a sense of place, of belonging, an innate need to make this place the best that it can be, and therefore helping all the people that choose to live here."

What is a significant contribution(s) you have made to community building?

(With Laura, there is never one answer, and never a short response!) "Communication; outreach; resource development; information assimilation; event organization; I'm a connector."

Why did you do this?

"I'm a helper; and when I see a need, I'm that 'somebody', as in 'somebody ought to do something about that …' OR, I know that somebody to help, or the team, etc. Fully subscribe to the mantra 'Be the change.'"

What talents and resources did (do) you use?

"The *Pioneer*; writing/PR skills, contacts, connection; marketing/advertising 30+ years of experience."

What does your community do well?

"Collaborate – working together – TEAM – Together Each Achieves More; strategic partnerships; because of the rural area, we have to work smarter with limited resources; we have to be innovative in our approaches and solutions."

What do people contribute to move this work ahead?

"My initial thought was 'not enough.' It's difficult to not be overwhelmed by how much work there is to do, and so many people that seem to just be sitting on the sidelines (and often complaining) about someone ought to do something'. But there are a couple of dozen (actually more than that – about 50) committed organizations and individuals that are moving things – but sometimes wonder about speed, direction, drivers, etc."

What is your role in community building?

"Getting the word out; Getting things done; Ideas; Contacts; it depends upon the project/organizations – what needs to be done; volunteer coordinator; fundraiser."

How do people view your role?

"My snarky answer would be you'd have to ask them … I would hope that people would view my role as 'vital' – as in, an integral part of the team, as in if you want your message out, I would be the go-to person."

Could you give me a one paragraph resume'?

"Laura Swanson – Editor/Partner with the *Tillamook County Pioneer*; Moved back to hometown on North Oregon Coast in 2002. A "born reporter" started career at local newspaper, "The *Fishrapper*", at age 15; continued as freelance correspondent, reporter and editor for variety of local, regional, national publications. Over 25 years in Portland metro area in advertising/marketing/PR for small/large advertising agencies. Established own ad/PR consulting business in 1990. Continue to work with a variety of clients in Portland Metro and local businesses, focus on nonprofits, agriculture, healthcare, tourism. Manzanita Farmers Market manager for eight years; Master Gardener; Avid outdoorswoman – enjoy gardening, camping, hunting, fishing; spending time with husband Rich and adult daughter/nursing student, Kalli and puppies, Kenai and Lucky.

You'll find Laura sitting at the table in important community committee meetings, speaking her mind, offering essential facts, making connections. She is also in the background at events, taking it all in, taking notes. You can see the wheels turning, as she is solving the puzzles, putting things together, thinking who needs to be connected to each other in order to move the project ahead.

She has that gift of long-range vision and planning. As a native, and as a relative to a large slice of the local population, she wants a better, healthier community. She has that "love of place", not only the natural beauty and the serenity that provides a sense of peace and healing to people, but a profound and deep love of the people here.

She knows all too well the ravages of poverty, hopelessness, loneliness and addiction. Her reporter mind seeks to investigate, inform and advance the thinking of the community on these vital issues.

The *Pioneer* and Laura's community work in all of her various "portfolios" is grassroots. She's a gardener, working the soil, weeding and planting, fertilizing and harvesting a variety of vegetables. She lives close to the land, out in the country, having close relationships with the forest, rivers, birds, and all the other riches of a healthy and productive natural world.

Her stories and her work are grassroots, too. She talks with and writes about real people and their lives, what they really struggle with, what their challenges are.

One day, we talked deeply of addiction and the ravages we have each seen in the ones we love, in the community; how lives have been upheaved. She trusts that people are generally inherently good, and that addiction is a disease, a parasitic plague that attacks people who are vulnerable.

"No one wakes up one morning and says, 'I'll think I'll be a drug addict'. Addiction is insidious, vicious, and non-selective, random," she says.

Tears well up in her eyes as she talks about the ravages of addiction. There are flashes of anger about how some components of the health care system have acted, often with indifference and callousness. The tears are replaced with fire, as she gets into a rant about care givers who don't seem to care, about a broken system that doesn't meet the underlying needs of those most vulnerable.

She's well versed on trauma-informed care, and has done her research, and ties it in to her own experiences in life, and the many stores she has heard from loved ones, neighbors, and friends. Being the investigative reporter, she has done her homework, and more, studying the issue carefully and thoroughly.

Like any of her news stories, she shows passion and human interest, being thorough yet engaging in the telling. She draws you in, making you feel that you can be part of the solution, part of the conversation on what will make a difference in her beloved community.

"It's not rocket science," I can hear her say.

It's all about relationship, about connection, about ending isolation and that dreadful, almost fatal attitude of hopelessness and failure. She's a believer in self action, and self-initiation of change.

Being rural isn't really a limitation. Rural and isolation are not absolutes, not the determining factors in failure. Being rural and isolated means we have to depend on ourselves to do the work, to do the heavy lifting. And, because we have strong relationships, because we are resilient and independent, stubborn people, we are the true change agents, the real movers and shakers.

"There is a path forward," I can imagine her saying. She is a guiding light for that work.

8 TEENS IN ACTION

What's a teenager to do on a school holiday that is unseasonably warm and sunny? Attend an improvisational theatre workshop of course.

Seven Tillamook High School students engaged in a three-hour workshop with performing arts teacher Bobi Burgh at the Fairview Grange on Veterans' Day. They immediately began role playing, improvising, and taking on dozens of characters, performing scenes and skits on a wide range of spontaneous topics.

Many of the students were part of Burgh's Black Box Theatre Academy at Tillamook High School, an innovative after school program that welcomes personal creativity, spontaneity, humor and drama. Playing a variety of characters, including animals and mythical creatures, the students continually challenged themselves and their peers in expanding their creative dramatic skills.

Burgh, an experienced director and teacher, kept offering fresh commands and direction, keeping the teens fully engaged and "on the mark" during the three-hour workshop. They often broke into small groups and solo events, continually acting and improvising.

The event was sponsored by the Fairview Grange, funded by grants from the THS Charity Drive and the Braemer Family Trust. Much of the grant revenue will be used by the Grange to purchase a new sound system for the historic 1916 stage and performance hall, the scene of monthly open mics, and a variety of community events.

THS students are no strangers to the Fairview Grange stage, with several of the THS choir groups performing their repertoire during the school year. Other student music and theatre groups, including the Oregon Coast Children's Theatre, are planning to use the Grange as a performance venue.

Several of the students, new to improv, said their excitement and enjoyment of the day will lead them to join the fun at the Black Box Theatre Academy.

The Black Box Theatre Academy teaches empathy, compassion, and understanding. There is a great deal of education that goes on, with kids developing skills and confidence that will change their lives. They are doing things, acting out roles, finding confidence in doing something they may not have imagined doing a year ago, finding their voice and drawing upon talent that has been hidden, lying dormant, and unappreciated, unrecognized.

A good teacher brings that out in students, giving them space to showcase their talent, building their confidence, and pushing them in the right direction.

"What is your gift? What is your talent? What are you capable of?"

These are the questions of the day. Not directly asked but implied in the assignments. Risking yourself in front of others, edging out on a limb to do something you didn't think possible. Risking embarrassment, awkwardness, uncertainty. Trying something new. Challenging yourself to take on a role, express emotion, and maybe look foolish in the process.

Everyone else here is risking that same feeling: embarrassment, social awkwardness, trying something new. You are among friends; we are all taking a risk.

In this class, you are expected to take risk, to try something new, daring. Daring to find yourself, to expose your gifts, and be expressive. Here, creativity and imagination are valued, cherished. The Grange hall is a safe place, away from the chaos and noise of school, hundreds of other students who may find it easy to laugh at you, mock you, even bully you for trying something new and challenging.

The teacher joins in, demonstrating, modeling, coaching. She is your friend, your ally, your model and coach. The strongest feeling in the room is trust. Step out on a limb and I will support you and I will applaud you. Take the dare and live in the moment.

Everyone else joins in, too. There are no slackers, no obvious hesitation. Everyone takes the risk, expands their imagination and moves ahead, being actors, letting down their barriers and going with the flow.

This is an exercise in personal courage. A day off from school, when you could take advantage of the unseasonable sunlight and warmth, going to the beach with friends, relaxing, taking a break from the daily routine. Or, you could be here in this Grange hall, taking risks, maybe be embarrassed, humiliated. But, instead, you find everyone else here supporting you, watching your back, adding to the moment, the experience by throwing you a line, joining in on the dialogue, interacting with your character, to deepen the dialogue, and move the plot of the skit forward, as if you've been collaborating and co-writing the screen play for weeks.

This is all ad lib, spontaneous, going with your gut. The few words of the teacher's prompt not even a skeleton of what you are creating here, forming your character, adding some drama, and moving the plot you've developed forward.

When you get lost, and the creative energy breaks, the teacher calls out "curtain" and the skit is done, completed. There is closure, and a completion of the burst of energy you've created in the room.

Quickly, you all move on to the next scene, the next experience, barely having enough time to take a breath and regroup. Go, go, go, the teacher seems to say, insisting you dig into the energy in your gut and keep creating, keep acting and imagining.

The lesson here is that there are no limits, no barriers to your creative spirit, that the impossible is just a concept, but not necessarily your reality. You are capable of anything, and you know that truth, you feel it inside of yourself, that feeling is embedded in your heart and your soul.

How wonderful, at sixteen, to realize that you have unlimited potential, that you are a creative, empowered and talents spirit. That your dreams have no limits, except the ones you place on them, artificially and arbitrarily.

"It is essential to self-discovery that we do get lost sometimes, because that's what encourages resourcefulness, builds confidence, and makes room for the unexpected." --- Carolyn Hax, advice columnist (2019)

The pace of the workshop is fast, and maybe some get lost here. It is a good lost, a rich moment in their creative lives. You need to feel that off balanced, uneasy feeling, as your struggle to regain your footing and find your foundation is, at first, unsettling, but it makes you grow, and it gives you the strength to deal with the unexpected, the unknown.

From that unsettling, you test yourself and you gain agility and balance.

"I can do this," you say to yourself, as you meet these challenges and grow.

Somehow, the teacher keeps up with the adolescent energy of the seven students. She is quicker to think on her feet than the students are. The observer thinks this isn't her first experience with kids, and with these activities, as her toolbox, her imagination seems unlimited. She knows when to prod, when to praise, and when to slightly change the plan. She moves them ahead, sensing when they need to be challenged and when they need to reflect on what they are doing, and how they've managed to move themselves ahead, and find themselves outside of their comfort zone.

In this work, there is a great deal of laughter and smiles.

"We are here to have fun," the teacher says in a pause in the work. "Just have fun and be in the moment," she reminds them.

Pizza has arrived and the aroma fills the room, reminding them that two and a half hours have gone by in a flash, and they are hungry. There are a few jokes about food and pizza and theatre, and some more laughter.

The teacher coaxes them into a few more skits and routines, urging them on, saying she's seeing some real growth and progress, that they are good actors, with tons of talent. She throws out a few more prompts and redivides the group into new dyads and triads of young talent. New skits are quickly developed, and the students take turns being the audience and the actors. The "fourth wall" of Brecht quickly forms in the hall, and new theatrical energy fills the room. Lines are spoken, gestures made, people are in motion, quickly entrapping the rest of us into the sense we are on a stage in a major theatre, and great theatre is being performed right in front of our eyes.

There are thousands in the audience, and a first class, sold out production is underway. We are in that magical moment that only theatre can create.

We are caught up in the moment, the performance, and the very short story is told, engaging us in the dialogue, the movements, the gestures and expressions. No costumes, no props except for a few folding metal chairs and a wooden floor, are present, except in our minds. That magic is created, and we are all enraptured.

In a few moments, the skits have ended, and we have applauded, the actors taking their bows, and the room fills with woops of excitement and words of congratulation and glee. Laughter rings out, and high fives are given. The last curtain seems to fall, and the house lights come up, as all of the plays and skits and performances come to a close.

I find myself unsure of reality, my mind still back in the moment, the worlds created by the students, as they wove their magic into a theatrical presence with me.

The workshop comes to an end, and the pizza boxes are opened, normal high energy teenaged chatter filling the room. We crowd around the table, the actors devouring the pizza with zeal and newfound appetites. Conversation around the table centers on their excitement, of past performances and the feelings generated by this morning of devotion and hard work. They talk of school and navigating the social interactions of adolescence, and the joy of finding something creative that they can identify with and celebrate.

They joke with their teacher, who now just seems to be the respected peer at one end of the table. There is familiarity yet deep respect for her abilities and her devotion to them and their artistic growth.

Parents come, the student sharing the thrill of their morning, their stories of success and wonder at what was created, what the teacher was able to call from them, on this otherwise unremarkable Monday morning.

Soon, they wander off, seemingly focused on the next activity of the day, willing to leave this experience with some silence, letting it soak into their souls, and enrich their lives without a convenient or certain measure.

9 --- BRIDGE BUILDING

Twenty-five of us in a circle, from two counties, spread out over a hundred plus miles of coastline, from up the Columbia River to almost a third of the way down the Oregon coast. Every one of us knows about ten others, and now, we are together, ready to get to know everyone here, and do something.

We've committed to four Sunday afternoons being together, talking about community building, strengths and weaknesses, and how we can live in community together. "Building Bridges" the two facilitators tell us.

We've had to apply for our seats in this circle, apparently chosen for our talents and work in the community, as "builders" and voices. It's an Oregon Humanities project, funded by a grant from the Oregon Community Foundation. We are to dive deep into rural communities and talk about how to make our lives and our communities healthier, more vibrant, more sustainable. How to have difficult conversations, how to "meet in the middle" and bridge divides, finding unity and commonality.

"When we think of "divides," many of us think of a familiar story, one that we hear in conversations with neighbors, see on the

Internet, and read in the news. It goes like this: we are a nation, a state, a community divided—politically, racially, ethnically, economically, geographically, and generationally. But the truth is more complicated.

"At Oregon Humanities, we explore this complexity by convening groups regionally throughout the state to talk together about the fractures and connections we experience in our communities.

"Bridging Oregon participants explore the ways we are divided by our life experiences and circumstances, the ways we are connected, and how we can deepen relationships with one another to create stronger, more resilient communities." —

https://www.oregonhumanities.org/programs/bridging-oregon/

As we go around the circle and introduce ourselves and talk about a special object each of us brought, something that represents our connection to the north Oregon coast, we soon find commonality and shared passion among us. We coalesce, sharing experiences, and begin to bond with each other, forming a group.

We're all verbal, opinionated, forceful, easily provoked into action and getting something done. We renew connections with old friends, old community partners, and make new relationships.

There's some trust in the room already. We take tentative steps to develop more of that essential, and start to work together, working our chemistry. Our facilitators pick up on our momentum and try to keep ahead of us, leading us into coalition building and bonding. They sense we are already doing that, without much need of coaching, and they step away at times, letting us do our work, letting us start to shape ourselves into a new, organic and living entity.

What will this look like when we are done? We'll grow as a group and individually.

We will "explore topics relevant to (our) region, address how (our) differences and perceived and real divides inform (our) experiences, and consider connections with one another now and into the future."
https://www.oregonhumanities.org/programs/bridging-oregon/

Yet, I suspect the journey will be more inspiring and informative than our pre-conceived idea of what the end will look like.

We are asked to be visionaries, bringing our talents and our experiences to the circle. Pearls of wisdom abounded:

—Am I clear on my intention for what it is that I want to happen here?

—What is the common welfare?

—Talking about the hard stuff

—"But when you change anything, anything at all, it gives people standing to complain." —Kevin Washburn, former Assistant Secretary to the Department of Interior for Indian Affairs.

—Meeting in the middle

—Trust

—How to unite us

—The heart of my life is living on the coast

—A time to talk with people who are different than me.

—People can be engrossed and attached to their story, not listening to others' stories.

—How do we connect to that animosity?

—How do we connect to that other story?

—Growth can be uncomfortable.

—Being not able to go beyond your own circle

—How do you break out of your own circle?

—How do you break into someone else's circle?

—I will converse with you, but not when there is a denial of my humanity or a negation of my values.

—How to allow differences to exist, yet not deny who you are?

—The discrepancy between intention and effect

There are two choices: the inside work, what goes on in me, and the changes in me, and the outside work, being in community, giving to and changing the community

Or, we can do both.

Smaller is often better.

Our work is to channel our emotional energy, often through art.

This group and its formation are somewhat artificial, initiated by an organization from elsewhere, and not formed by an immediate crisis or situation. We don't have a tangible, definable problem to solve. We've been invited to the circle not because of particular problem-solving skills for a task at hand, or an identifiable role in the problem. Rather, we are "ad hoc", and undefined.

We are limited to three more sessions, and then, perhaps, we agree to continue, or morph into something more structured, focused.

Time will tell, and an adventure awaits.

Meeting Again

"The greatness of a community is more accurately measured by the compassionate actions of its members." -- -Coretta Scott King

"We cannot seek achievement for ourselves and forget about progress and prosperity for our community. ... Our ambitions must be broad enough to include the aspirations and needs of others, for their sakes and for our own." --- Cesar Chavez.

The second session of the "Building Bridges" work group, facilitated by Oregon Humanities, began slowly, the rainy, foggy day delaying travel, yet sharpening our collective desire to come back together, and delve into community dynamics and our common desire to take on some hard issues. Yet, we first needed to again explore how we look at this work, and how we, as a group, can agree on how we do our work.

We are clearly leaders in our respective communities, leaders in opinion shaping, in conversations, and in exploring solutions.

"Leadership is not being in charge; it is about taking care of people in your charge." Simon Sinek.

The quote, spoken by one of our members, hung in the air. We were uncharacteristically silent for a few minutes, contemplating what that meant. We are caretakers, guardians and nurturers of our fellow humans, and acting as leaders in those roles. In that broad definition then, isn't everyone a leader, as we are all caregivers of others?

I carefully wrote down the quote, finding myself needing to ponder it more, in the quiet of the early morning, when the mysteries of the universe required my contemplation.

The topic today was digging into the metaphor of bridges, in terms of community function and improvement.

The person next to me in our circle reminded us that we all drove over bridges to be here today, many small bridges, spanning creeks and marshes. We drove over bigger bridges, too, over rivers and bays. In our lives in our community, we are also the users of bridges, built by those who came before us, who built bridges when they were needed, satisfying needs and accomplishing purposes, which, today, we likely just take for granted.

"Not a problem; there's already a bridge."

Perhaps we need to be mindful of those bridges, and the intentions they have served.

We dove into group dynamics, again asking how we work as a group, working with tough problems and coming together as problem solvers and vocalizing community values. How often do we really examine how we relate to others and talk about tough social issues?

One member spoke of her community's struggle to find unity. There was a controversial issue on the recent ballot on funding a new city hall in the small town. The issue split the community, with heated public meetings, and personal attacks. The results defeated the measure, some seeing it as a no confidence vote for the mayor and city council. The underlying problem remains, an old, inadequate city hall, and the city now heavily invested in a large piece of property without a bond to build a new city hall.

Wise people held a healing service, sponsored and led by all of the community's churches, beginning with rituals of unity candles and prayers for contemplation, forgiveness and understanding. The focus was on hope and aspirations, and love of the community.

Another member related her community's anguish over an issue facing the board of a local non-profit. The controversy seemed ludicrous to an outsider, but the controversy and the conflicting stories and rumors continue to be divisive and antagonistic. Friendships are being lost and the atmosphere in the community is "on edge", putting years of good work for the goals of the non-profit at risk. The social fabric is frayed.

That member contrasted that challenge, that community agony, with her praise for the local school system. The schools celebrate and model diversity and acceptance, on what were previously deeply divided opinions about homosexual relationships and interracial marriage. A significant factor is that the school employees who might have been, in an earlier age, targets of racism and homophobia, are "homegrown" and have deep family connections and relationships in the community. It is not "outsiders" who are imposing their values and lifestyles on the community, but people who have grown up there, who have deep and personal ties with a broad spectrum of the community.

The conversation moved to the topic of the day: bridges, a metaphor for the work that we already do and the work we need to be doing to strengthen and build community.

A long and deep discussion ensued, in small groups, as we brainstormed what a bridge really is, and how bridging gaps and differences as well as commonalities, can both strengthen and divide a community. Ideas flew around the room as we regrouped:

First, we build small bridges, so we know how to build bigger bridges.

Are the first bridges we need to build within ourselves, bridging our spirituality with our daily lives, connecting within ourselves? And, then move on to build the bridges within our partnerships, our families, our neighbors, and then our communities? Does that extend on to regions, nations, the world?

What is the function of a bridge? Is it to span a gap, a chasm, or is it really a device to allow us to invade, conquer, and vanquish another culture, another viewpoint? Is a question of dominance or unification?

Connection --- does that term need re-defining? Are we tying together what has been separate? Is that good or bad? A community bridge may be a new whole.

In bridges, there is an engineering term, the "key". In a stone bridge or arch, this is the vital stone at the top, a wedge, that actually binds the bridge together, giving it greater strength, and acts as a unifying force. We should explore that concept of a key, both a wedge and a unifier, a strengthener.

Building a bridge is something one person cannot do. It takes a group, with a common purpose, and a variety of skills. What one does affects the whole, a bringing together, a sharing.

The idea of the bridge comes before the making of the bridge, and there must be an agreement to build the bridge, and then, together, and using our individual skills, to create the bridge.

A bridge project needs a visionary, a leader of the project, architects, engineers, a variety of skilled builders, people having a variety of talents and skills, sharing a common vision. There must be intention, an asking of how that intention is envisioned as well as received.

What are the properties of a bridge? What are its elements? What are we trying to bridge? What materials and knowledge are needed? Will this work then answer the question of why do we need this bridge?

How does the bridge then move out into the world, and serve its purposes? Does the bridge serve more than the community?

A bridge is connection, a span, spanning, movement, a conduit, a convener, balance, strength. A bridge is an above and a below space, a here and there thing, a sum of the whole of all of its parts. A bridge is both a divider and a unifier. A bridge can express unity and be a series of components.

We were left to mull all of this over, to return to our communities and contemplate the issue of bridges in our community. What bridges DO we have in our community? What are their purposes? Why were they built and how are they maintained? Is there a need for them now? Do they serve a legitimate purpose?

What bridges are needed? And what purpose would they have, what needs would be satisfied by the building of new bridges? Who would be the visionary, the leader, the architect, the engineers, the builders? How would the community be served? How would the community be strengthened and improved? Or would there be negative effects as well, if we built that bridge? How would the bridge be maintained?

A bridge may have unintended consequences. A bridge may advance fear and discomfort and provide a different method of engagement. Different bridges may not be accessible to all, but instead be restrictive, class-oriented, biased against those who are disfavored and lack power. A bridge may instead foster conflict and dominance.

A bridge can span a gap and have multiple uses and actions. How is the bridge used? A bridge is a part of a greater whole, and how can that be good, or bad? For whom?

A bridge may require acceptance, both conditionally and unconditionally. This may require both inner work, within our minds and souls, and outwardly with others, involving relationships and social interaction dynamics.

We should consider the forces around us, consulting with the architects and the engineers, to worry about the outside forces affecting the bridge. The question we ask is to consider additional strengths to the bridge, dealing with the unexpected, and the unique demands that this particular bridge, for what this particular job and location, would be required to withstand and meet.

A bridge may become its own entity, having its own unique, specialized existence, being a product of environment and need. Adding the bridge to the community changes community dynamics and adding to what people interact with in their lives. A bridge will change our thinking and our problem-solving methodologies.

Collaborating on a bridge requires many skills, many viewpoints and voices. Should everyone be involved, consulted, engaged? Or is the bridge the work of a few, and how would that change the nature of the bridge, its function and its role in the community?

Imagination requires imagining and imagining without consequences.

We need to be aware of the past, the history of past successes and failures, of development and change. The present is built upon the ruins and the foundations of the past. We are shifting the foundations of what we are building upon, and our awareness of that history, of what worked and what didn't, and why, and be better builders.

We often build bridges with a sense of urgency, worrying about time and change, and the needs of the present. Yet, be mindful of the past and the future.

In bridge building, there is tension. Tension can come from anger, and bringing things and ideas together, with conflict and anxiety and the apparent lack of workable solutions. In that messy process, there can be found strength and solutions. Tension is like a fire, tempering the steel in the forge, making for a better, stronger, more durable, more usable tool.

A bridge can also have ductability, the characteristic of being flexible, pliable, yet with a strength and resolve; bending with the wind, but not breaking.

A bridge has utility and equality. Every part is important, and essential. Without all of the components, and without all things being intrinsically strong and viable, the bridge is weakened and may fail.

We acknowledged the impact of bridge building, gaining some attributes and losing others. We need to be intentional and mindful of such choices and consequences. Every act has a result, intended or otherwise. What are we doing here? Building for the common good and better lives, or not? Maybe what we see as benefits of bridge building will really be detriments for the community.

We need time to ponder all of this, to be mindful, thoughtful, and pensive. Time may be on our side if we hit the "pause" button and contemplate, weighing the pros and cons, and doing some deep imagining and analysis.

Meeting Again

We make a list of the words, the ideas that we have been wrestling with in the past two months:

Energy

Community

Unity

Growth

Community life

Not contentious

Harmonizing

Connection

Regard for others

Each person has a different place where we start. We can start anywhere --- all strengths and gifts are equally important. Do we have to have an outcome, a product? No. We measure success in other ways. We move forward.

I may not see my reward. That action is what is important, what makes a difference.

(A redefinition of success – it is a calling.)

Perhaps new language is called for.

It is something that cannot be quantified, it is without attachment to an outcome.

How do my actions fit into the actions of a group? I am involved in a process.

We need to find our sounding board group, people who support me in this work, who encourage, recognize the struggles, my talents, my efforts, yet suspend judgement and simply be supportive of what I am doing, my involvement in a process.

I need my support group to move me towards asking the next best question.

When I am in pain, I need to have beauty.

We need to keep our experiences alive in some form. We are all connected; we all have our own stories. We need to heal from and to learn from our own stories.

If you are not part of the solution, you are part of the problem. But this idea may be a burden. Be less burdened by seeing yourself as part of the process, to be perseverant.

Honor our willingness to keep our own lights lit.

Indicators of success are not necessarily measurable, quantifiable. Rather, we should strive for a list of qualities.

The poet Stanley Kunitz writes, hearing a voice from the clouds:

"...

'Live in the layers,

not on the litter.'

Though I lack the art

to decipher it,

no doubt the next chapter

in my book of transformations

is already written.

I am not done with my changes."

Layers, Stanley Kunitz

The process, by us being involved, committed, immersed in this work, will change us.

We have been asked to bring an object to this gathering, as an expression of where we are at in this work, where we are at in ourselves. I bring two talking sticks, gifting them to our two leaders as we gather in circle.

10 --- THE TALKING STICK

When people gather with the intention of talking about a serious issue, what are the rules of engagement? As a society, we have common assumptions and expectations on how we conduct our business, how we proceed, how we act together.

Or, maybe we don't anymore. Maybe we only hang out with those we generally agree with and ambush the "others" on social media with snarky comments and end up not really listening to people or engaging with them in meaningful conversations and problem-solving.

I am often not sure of the "rules" anymore. Looking to national leadership, those politicians and media massagers have perfected the 30 second sound bite, something that fits into the time pressures of a newscast or a quick quip that can be endlessly repeated on a social media "news feed".

Often, that isn't news but well-crafted propaganda and, according to many, "fake news".

I rebel against such thinking and practice. We can do better.

In many cultures, there is an ancient custom that promotes listening, respect, and democratic (with a small "D") conversation and decision-making. Some call it intelligent discourse.

The talking stick is a hand-crafted physical object, literally a stick fashioned from wood and adorned with various artistic additions, an object of beauty and craftsmanship. The stick is passed around a circle of people gathered for a common purpose. The person who holds the stick "has the floor". Others are silent and the holder of the stick speaks in a room of respectful and sacred silence, to express their opinions, views, and feelings.

There are no interruptions, snippy comments, groans or accolades. Instead, the person is free to speak their peace, and then hand off the talking stick to the next person, who has the same rights and is treated to the same respect and deference.

In many of such groups that I've been privileged to be a part of, those who are shy or otherwise reluctant to speak receive respect and attention. Their views are valued and listened to. Everyone has the same right to be heard and to not be interrupted.

Part of this conversational work is to "check in", to say out loud how life has been going, to say where we are at with our emotions and thoughts, how life is treating us, and how we are doing in navigating the world and our society. The talking stick protocol compels all of us to listen, pay attention, and let the speaker pause if need be, letting silence also be a voice, and to bring us closer to each other.

When we listen, and use the talking stick, we find unity and communion. The physical space we are in as a group also becomes a spiritual space, a safe place. And, healing occurs, a place for catharsis and shedding of shame and guilt. Perhaps a time for confession, and always a time for acceptance and being loved and honored for who we are.

It becomes a space for speaking our Truth.

One of the rules is confidentiality. What is said in the circle stays in the circle. We have agreed not to gossip, not to share others' tragedies and struggles with others in the community who are outside of our circle. Personal safety and respect are valued. Often, the silence also sends messages, and builds our trust and our relationship with each other.

I am not alone. I have colleagues, friends, companions who respect me and the words that I speak. There is a sense of belonging, that I am valued, and that others are also valued and have an important role in my life.

Such a place, within a sacred circle, where being given room to speak freely and without being judged by others, is a rarity in our world. I cherish that time together, a place "outside" of the normal "rules of engagement", where weakness and vulnerability is often then used by others to gain advantage in the various subcultures of society. Many of us appropriate such revelations and disclosures for gossip and gaining an upper hand against someone else. The lesson becomes "don't be honest and open, for that is weakness and will be used against you."

This week, I make talking sticks. I am in this new group, with rules and expectations that are still tender but are coming into place. People are yearning for a sense of community, a sense of wanting to be in this group. I sense the need for a talking stick, to help guide our conversations, to build a sense of the sacred and of community.

I find myself on the riverbank, looking for the right stick shaped by the forest and the water. I go to the beach, being open for what the ocean has caused to appear on the beach, to adorn and add to the stick. I add paint, and oils and other decorations, as symbols of nature and community. This process has no formal rules or rubrics, only my sense of space and what is needed for this particular talking stick and the work we are doing together. Some would call this an "organic" process, outside of formalities and restrictions of our society.

I call it peacemaking.

I speak in the circle, holding these new talking sticks, and offer them as gifts to our leaders, who have given much to us and this process. They hold them in silence, emotional, and excited. In a few minutes, our discussion on values and motives and self-awareness continues. As people signal their desire to contribute to the conversation, a talking stick is passed to them, and, soon, is passed on to the next speaker. There is no verbal acknowledgement of the talking stick and its role in our conversation, yet, the talking stick has been accepted, and incorporated into our work. Each holder grasps the stick, feeling it, and sensing its power and its new role in our group.

The peacemaking continues.

11 --- THE IMPACT OF LIBRARIES

Public libraries have had a profound impact on American life, being a cornerstone for public education, social interaction, and community well-being.

The first American public library began in Philadelphia, with Benjamin Franklin and others donating books and creating a lending library.

Today, there are 16,568 public libraries in the United States, a number greater than the number of Starbucks cafés, with more than 1.4 billion visits a year. Americans made 113 million visits to library programs in 2018, greater than attendance at all professional sporting events. (https://ala.org).

Libraries are community centers, fulfilling essential roles not only in the availability of printed materials, but also on-line data bases, e-books, magazines and research materials. Children's books and audio-visual materials are readily available, and home-schooled kids are able to enjoy an unlimited supply of materials.

Wi-fi is almost universally available. In our community, a fourth of the population lack computers and internet access at home and the library is a major source of access for them.

"In a recent keynote address to the American Association of Law Librarians, Georgetown University law professor Shon Hopwood explained how a library saved his life.

"Hopwood told the story of how, at age twenty-three, he was convicted of armed bank robbery and sentenced to twelve and a half years in federal prison. While there, a fellow inmate gave him a chance to work in the prison library. As he shelved books, he became interested in their contents and began reading the law. He taught himself how to advocate, and how to file petitions. Other inmates began consulting him about their legal problems, and eventually, he succeeded in having two petitions granted by the US Supreme Court. These and other efforts led to legal victories for the inmates he advocated for, including substantial sentence reductions. His exceptional skills as an advocate brought him to the attention of the legal profession. …"

He served his sentence, went to law school and passed the Bar.

"It all began in the library. According to Hopwood, the law library gave him the freedom to pursue learning, it broke his self-centeredness and enabled him to focus on helping others, and it nurtured his confidence that he could succeed. It was the one element in the prison environment that contradicted the daily message that 'you [the prisoner] are garbage and you'll be back.' It saved his life.

"Yet prison libraries are chronically under-funded. According to the US Bureau of Prison, it cost over $36,000 to incarcerate each inmate in the Federal prison system in fiscal year 2017. (Federal Register, April 30, 2018)." (https://ala.org)

Why I Love the Library

My hometown library and I go way back. We are best friends.

One of my earliest memories was going with my mom to the "old" library, before I could read. We'd walk up the ramp to the second floor of the old city hall building, the hardwood floors creaking with age. I still recall that smell of floor wax and old books.

We'd find so many books for my mom and my dad to read to me at bedtime, books about anything I was curious about. Our visits were just part of our life, and books became a treasured part of my life. If there was ever a question around the dinner table, someone would say, "Let's look into that at the library".

Mom, Dad and my brothers checked out books, too. The library was a big part of our family life.

The library moved across the street when the old library simply outgrew itself. The vacant car dealership became our library, with more room for books and study tables, even a corner for kids and weekly story times. The town was very proud of our new library.

On a warm spring day, my first-grade class paraded the six blocks to the library, where we all got our brand-new library cards. I still have mine and remember the "ka-thunk" sound it made in the check-out machine at the front desk.

My own library card! The world opened up to me, and I explored the stacks and the card catalog. Sometimes, the librarian would show me a new book that had come in, knowing I'd be interested.

The summer reading program was one of the highlights of my childhood. I kept a stack of books on my bedside table, a habit I carry on today.

In high school, the library was the place to meet friends downtown, and the place to research and write papers, and keep checking out books.

When I was in college, I'd stop by to work on a paper, and visit with the librarians, who asked me how school was going, and what I'd been reading.

The library continued to be a part of my life, and I kept up with my reading, and finding materials I needed for my law practice. I'd send clients there for books, even helping folks become cardholders and lifelong readers like me.

Yet, the "new" library was bursting at the seams. There wasn't enough room for new books, and the "story hour" area was pushed up against the study tables filled with high school students and everyone else who came to check out a book.

The new librarian, Sara Charlton, started the conversation about dreaming of a new library, and the idea took off.

The voters agreed, and, for the first time, we had a community library that was actually designed as a library. Spacious, well-lit, and supplied with an abundance of study rooms and community activity rooms, the library opened its doors in 2006.

Our main library is the crown jewel of our county library system, joining community-supported libraries in Manzanita, Rockaway Beach, Garibaldi, Bay City, and Pacific City.

Those branch libraries are housed in buildings owned and maintained by independent community organizations, with the library system supplying the staff and materials for a vibrant library system. Each library offers materials and services to meet the needs of their community.

The bookmobile continues to be an essential part of our "library life" in our county, visiting neighborhoods, schools, community centers, and homes throughout the county, offering library resources to everyone.

Our Tillamook County library system attracts nearly 200,000 visits a year, with over 400,000 items being checked out. The library offers not only books and children's story times, but e-books, other on-line materials, language education, music, and movies for all. Free programs offer a full range of experiences and educational opportunities. Computer access gives people job searching and research opportunities that are convenient and free.

I still hear people tell each other, "I'll meet you at the library."

The idea of what is a library has grown tremendously from what I experienced as a first grader. Today, libraries have a much greater, more diverse role in our community, meeting needs unheard of sixty years ago. I'm proud that our library continues to be a vigorous, forward thinking center of our community.

68% of my neighbors are library users, and nearly all of us believe the library does a great job serving the community.

My little paper library card with the metal tab, the one that made the check-out machine go "ka-thunk" back in the 1960s has been replaced with a plastic bar-coded card. Computers and self-check scans, and a new generation of highly skilled librarians have brought the library into the 21st century. An automated check in machine has been installed, streamlining the librarians' work and giving them more time to interact with customers like me.

Art displays from local artists, including students, and attractive meeting and study rooms add to the welcoming atmosphere of the library. A variety of interesting programs entice people to the library, offering fresh perspectives and experiences. The phrase "community center" now defines our library.

From my reading chair at home, I can peruse the library catalog and order materials on my laptop, checking out e-books, and studying another language, or simply satisfying my curiosity about something.

Still, I have my good conversations with the librarians about new books, new materials, and the cheery "here's something you might be interested in". My curiosity about the world when I first visited the library when I was a toddler continues today, and the library keeps offering me a key to the world.

And, around the dinner table or at the coffee shop, when a question comes up, someone is still quick to say, "let's look into that at the library".

12---- SEARCHING FOR A DESTINATION

"I think it was Brene Brown who told a story about a village where all the women washed clothes together down by the river. When they all got washing machines, there was a sudden outbreak of depression and no one could figure out why.

"It wasn't the washing machines in and of themselves. It was the absence of time spent doing things together. It was the absence of community." —Sacred Dreams (Facebook, 2019)

What makes a community, and how can I strengthen that?

I keep coming back to that fundamental question, and the role I can have in being a builder, a steward of community.

Throughout humanity's history, we have lived in and built community. As hunters and gatherers on the African plains, in our journeys to the rest of the world, and our evolution from nomadic, hunter-gatherer societies into a more agrarian societies, and creating villages, towns, and cities, a central commonality is that we are communal, a collective of talents and personalities, sharing our skills and working and living together.

In that work, we have developed family structures, religions, technologies, and laws that help unite us, focusing on common purpose and a generalized sense of "us". Our rituals and the patterns of our daily lives weave us together, and we find strength and purpose in our commonalities.

Language, music, and the other arts emerged, giving us tools to express our innermost selves, and to celebrate our commonalities as well as our individualities. Our diversities enriched our lives and our culture. When we honor and strengthen our individual talents and gifts, our collective lives also develop depth and rich complexity.

When our farmer ancestors gathered together to trade their harvests and ensure an abundant store of food for the coming winter, stories were told, wisdom was shared, and common bonds were established and strengthened.

Today, the challenges aren't in developing technology to communicate and inform; those tools are overwhelmingly abundant, to the point that we find ourselves absorbed in our "screen life", and don't really know our neighbors or live socially in our villages and cities. We can easily enjoy culture from the comfort of our couches, at the expense of interacting with those around us.

One can easily feel the loneliest in the midst of a busy, crowded coffee shop operated by multi-national corporations, with menus and customer service models developed without considering the uniqueness and "flavor" of the neighborhood.

Even the commonalities and ties of a national culture are ebbing, as television networks news and sit-coms developed for the national and international audience have smaller audiences. People now have so many choices for viewing that we have much less in common to experience in our culture. At home, everyone can watch their own shows and engage in their own social media experiences, separate from everyone else in the same room.

Do these trends make for a less vibrant culture, weaker families and neighborhoods, or does this abundance of electronic "content" strengthen us, making us individually more sophisticated, and better equipped to maximize our individual talents and gifts?

Or, is it a choice between living abundantly in community or being better off individually? In a democratic, pluralistic society, I suggest that the answer is in duality. A richer, more abundant, more pluralistic society can also successfully enrich and cultivate individualistic abundance and diversity, which then enriches and broadens society.

This "cycling" of societal and individual resources and experiences isn't always smooth. There's tension and conflict, but such has always been the case in democratic societies, which is messy and sometimes confusing. Yet, culture advances and the depth of creativity and talent increases, for the benefit of all.

I can lament the absence of community building and opportunities to come together in my community, or I can be an instrument of change. Weep or act.

Several years ago, my wife and I decided to join the local Grange. There was a small group of good-hearted, focused people who were working to revive the Grange, keep the building open and make it, once again, a vibrant part of the community.

We wanted a better community, and we wanted a place where what we could contribute would make a difference. And, we wanted to improve our social life and our "connections" with others, and do that in a meaningful, productive way. As is true throughout America, the popular social settings involved alcohol, organized sports, "being seen" and idle chatter, or a deadly combination thereof.

We chuckled about being old fuddy-duddies, geezers. Our grandparents had been active in their Granges, complete with Saturday night dances, potlucks and Christmas bazaars. How old fashioned!

Yet, for our ancestor farmers, the Grange was one of the few places people could gather, visit, and do something fun. Politically, the Grange filled a vital role in the years after the Civil War. Farmers were exploited by railroads charging exorbitant shipping fees for their crops, and merchants would overcharge farmers for seeds, fertilizers and equipment.

The Grange movement quickly spread across the nation, and created its own insurance company, offering very competitive crop and casualty insurance to farmers. Grange halls were built as dance halls, with acoustically engineered stages, and venues for educational programs and potluck suppers. Weddings, funerals, political events and other community activities had a home, often in areas where the only community building was a one-room schoolhouse that would serve as a church on Sundays.

When television came on the cultural scene in the 1950s, and America turned to more "sophisticated" cultural activities, Granges declined. Yet, now we seem to be more in need of some local, small group socializing than ever before.

Two years ago, I had a conversation that has made a big difference in my life and has changed my community. Three of us, all Grange members, were sitting in the Grange hall. It was cold, dusty, and depressing. The years of neglect and indifference had taken its toll on the old building. We rented it out occasionally for events, but it was a sad place.

The three of us came from different walks in life. We had histories of being teachers, government officials, musicians, artists, parents, and community activists. We all loved working with kids and the struggles of improving the lives of young people and giving them opportunities.

Our conversation focused on how we could improve the lives of youth, and also the entire community, having a place for the creative and performing arts, a place where people could come together to play music, dance, show their art, and generally celebrate the good things that a community can offer. There needed to be a decent venue for weddings and funerals and anniversaries, and a place for organizations to hold a fund raiser and bring people together.

We quickly listed what was available in our community, and no place really got the five-star ranking for our energy to renovate and build a great community hall.

One of my buddies paused and looked around.

"Well," he said, and paused.

We paused and followed his gaze and looked around the hall.

"I think, my friends, we are looking at it. We're sitting in it."

"This is the place."

We chuckled, my buddy being the antithesis of a preacher, let alone Brigham Young.

Still, he had a point. The hall had been built in 1916, using the Grange architectural plans, that created an exquisitely acoustically balanced stage and hall in the days before electricity and microphones.

With some major cleaning, refurbishing and paint, the place could be restored. There were possibilities here, just needing some well-focused effort and determination.

We made a list, we contacted the work crew of the local youth prison, we scored free paint from the county recycling program, the local hardware store donated painting supplies and gave us a discount on the special varnish needed on the maple dance floor.

Twenty trips to the landfill later, and countless scrubbings, sanding, and sandwich making for the work crews, the place started to shine. About a thousand staples from decades of wedding and dance decorations were pulled out of the walls.

The dance floor, hand crafted in 1916 from Michigan maple, shined. We painted and scrubbed, washed the windows, and happily tossed out the drapes from the 1940s.

We looked at the ancient and inefficient heating system and wished for a miracle. A casual conversation with an employee of the local PUD public utility soon brought us into the world of grant writing, heat pump and LED lighting engineering, rebates, and loans. Within a few months, that seemingly Herculean task brought us a $27,000 heat pump system and LED lighting. We slashed our electric bill, the savings easily covering our loan payment to the PUD, and gave us a warm, well lit, and attractive Grange hall. And, miracle of miracles, you could enjoy the Grange without wearing your coat, stocking cap and gloves.

It seemed everyone wanted to help us out, and passers-by would cheer us on as we gave a fresh coat of paint to the outside and cleared away the blackberries. Our story was featured in the PUD's monthly magazine and new groups of renters signed up to rent the hall.

And, we began to have a monthly Open Mic.

The three of us, and many of the other Grange members and others in the community had wanted a place to gather, to share our poetry, our music, and generally have a comfortable, alcohol free place to gather.

We start out with a light supper. Some crockpots of homemade soup, bread, salad, and cookies. There's a donation jar at the corner by the plates and silverware, but we don't make a big deal out of it. People give what they can or what they want. And, sharing a simple meal with others around the tables on the dance floor, they can relax and enjoy the talent on the stage.

Open mics are organic in nature. We have an emcee, who starts us off with one or two of his songs and his guitar. There's a sign-up list, and anyone can get up on the stage and read a poem, sing a song, or tell a story. You get about five minutes to do your thing, and you are among friends. Most everyone hasn't performed much before, so being a "first timer" is par for the course.

People get shy around a microphone, but are soon caught up in the moment, as they share their creativity, and the audience responds. And, we see amazing talent, and are always delighted and surprised at what our friend can create. We see growth and confidence, and get caught up in the joy of sharing, and being together, in community.

Open Mic

A place of personal courage, testing

Out new ideas, new expressions, a new

Part of ourselves, making our private, secret inner work

Public, part of the community.

Giving what is inside ourselves some air, the stage

Intimidating, yet distinctly our own

Space, space to make a statement –

Welcomed by acceptance, community in open arms – a

Declaration of who we are, giving voice

To what has been stewing, churning, fermenting

Inside

Finding its wings, finding its audience

Being heard.

This old space, sacred, the past hundred years,

Here others stood here, sharing their souls, over the years,

Voices and music reverberating on old Grange Hall wood, generations past

Giving to the community, making community, building

Relationships, embolding ourselves, our art, our

Creations.

I grow, often against my will, on this stage, exposing my private

Self, shyness and private musings somehow

Put on hold.

13 --- -FUNERALS AND UNITY

"…you don't know what you've lost 'til it's gone." — Joni Mitchell, *Big Yellow Taxi* (song, 1970)

Today, I sat in one of the back pews at the funeral for a good friend. It was time to pay my respects to a good person, to honor her life, and to be with her family and her many friends.

For me, it was a time of celebration and reflection. I grieved, yet my mourning and sadness was brightened by the good memories, and of a life filled with family, care, and building community.

She had lived a long and full life, and it was time for her to go, and it was time to wish her Godspeed in her spiritual journey.

Others found solace in the familiar rituals of the funeral mass, the prayers, the songs, Communion, and the quiet conversations before and after the service in the foyer and on the steps of the church. And, afterwards, the luncheon in the parish hall, where the good stories would be told, and people would connect with each other, catching up on their lives and connecting. Her spirit was present, but I missed her laugh, the twinkle in her eye, and her ever-present work on connecting people and moving one of her projects forward. She was never bashful about asking for your assistance, you putting in a good word for something, or giving someone some help when they were in a tough spot.

She wasn't shy about asking for a favor for a person who was down on their luck and needed a hand up. That good work comes back to you, in spades. It came back to me when I asked her for some help for a young man in need of some kindness and acceptance. Years later, she told me that he turned out to be one of the best workers she'd ever had in her restaurant.

She wouldn't want me to be all weepy at her funeral, either. She'd want me to watch over her family, and give them hugs, and warm handshakes, just being their friend and showing up. Sometimes, the real communication isn't about saying something.

One can feel very alone in the midst of the congregation at a funeral. I detach from the rituals and find myself in a place of contemplation and gratitude for knowing the person, of sharing a community with them, and living life together. I'm introspective and full of thought about a person's life, our lives together, and where I go now with all this contemplative energy and thought.

Ministers often speak of regrets and sadness at a funeral, giving our collective pain and grief some names, and putting our emotions on the community table for all to see and hear about. I like that about funerals, a time where we come up close and personal with death, dying, grief and loss. Without that reminder, that discussion, we'll often sweep the whole weepy mess under the rug and try to go about our lives, pretending we haven't been affected, that we're not going to die either, and that all this can be safely ignored.

We hear a lot of talk about spirituality and God's love from the pulpit from people clad in robes, the messengers from God assuring us that we are loved, that death is part of life, and that our pain and suffering can be eased, even healed, if we place our lives with God and accept a version of spiritual salvation and remedy.

There's comfort in that, and the ritual of the event offers normalcy, predictability, and order.

Yet, my friend is gone now, perhaps moving on to another place on the cosmic plane, and I'm not sure I really want to be saved, converted, or even consoled.

A good cry and some gnashing of teeth and ripping of my garments, along with a good dose of ashes, may be more in line with what I need in the moment, to work my way through my feelings of loss, mortality, and posterity. I find that I need to go sit in my grief for a while, and absorb all that pain, to fully grieve my loss.

Putting on fancier clothes and sitting politely in a church for an hour is the polite thing to do but it isn't a good substitute for a good cry and some rather loud and angry words with the Creator. And, some much needed reflection on who I am, and what I'm doing with my life. I need that catharsis and that wrestling with the darkness and the ache of loss and finality.

I'm a pretty verbal person, but I clam up at a funeral, unable to chitchat about the weather or fishing, or what I've been up to lately. Other people are like that, too, and my friends I see a lot at funerals are more comfortable with a sentence or two of "I'm thinking of you" and "Take care", mixed in with some good hugs. That's when we really communicate, when we really come together and express what is in our hearts.

The latent accountant in me comes to the forefront, and I take inventory and do an accounting of what my late friend has given to me, how my life has changed. In that process, I find solace in the balance sheet, the assets that I've accumulated, and how the world has become a better place by their well-lived life.

This day, this time sitting in the back pew of the church, was a lesson in a well-lived life. She was a hard worker, the mother of many children, the builder of a farm, the entrepreneur who ran a busy restaurant, the driving force in the family fishing business. A child died before his time, lost at sea. There were other disasters and tragedies, and moments of achievement, and betterment for so many people she helped. In all that, the community surrounded her, in good times and bad, and loved her.

In her later years, she turned her energy into building her community, spearheading civil improvements, establishing a museum, teaching others about the roots and vitality of the community. She didn't seek the limelight, but sought out the quiet, one on one conversations, and the talks outside in the hallway during countless community meetings.

Several times, she called me, out of the blue, asking for me to do something, make a connection, impart a few words of wisdom, put an idea into motion. But, in reality, she was the connector and the instigator.

She could be sneaky, and I loved her for it. She almost always knew where she was going, in her role of community builder, and she was in it for the long haul. It was one person at a time, one conversation at a time. And she was patient. When you mix determination and patience, and a great sense of timing, you had her recipe for success. She'd get her way, maybe not today, but eventually, we would all end up in a place where she had planned for all of us to be.

She was powered by love and infected all of us with her zeal of living life to the fullest, with purpose and intention.

I'm messed up now, grief working its way through me, throwing me off kilter, irregular, disoriented, especially when I think I'm fine, I am moving on, I'll be alright. But, I'm not. I need my time to sit in ashes and wail. I need that time in the grocery store, when I see someone else who knew her well, and we silently give each other a hug.

This work of grieving, mourning is building community, a time of looking back, taking stock, and realizing the beauty of what has been built, and contemplating where we go from here.

14 – THE FAITH COMMUNITY

"Living our vocation to be protectors of God's handiwork is essential to a life of virtue; it is not an optional or a secondary aspect of our Christian experience." — Pope Francis, *Laudato si'* encyclical (2015)

"People of faith, particularly missionary faith, believe deeply in something a lot of secular people aren't so sure about: that all people are capable of profound change. They remain convinced that the right combination of argument, emotion, and experience can lead to life-altering transformations.   That, after all, is the essence of conversion." —- Naomi Klein, *On Fire* (2019)

Faith based organizations and actions are a profound and active part of community life. Religious belief and having a spiritual mission is the "fuel" for many in the community who connect with others and energize community activities.

Churches and other organizations provide a place for people to gather, to conduct ceremonies and hold community events. Weddings and funerals call people to gather, and to celebrate and mourn, and participate in the most significant emotional communal events.   There is the thread of "being in communion".

Religious groups also promote personal change and growth, through education and spiritual activities, study groups, worship services, coffee groups, and church suppers.

In response to the growing and increasingly devastating and fatal opioid epidemic, along with alcohol and other drug abuse, some churches are hosting AA and NA groups, and the Christian-oriented Celebrate Recovery. Recovery groups are becoming mainstream, ordinary church programs for their congregations and the community. These churches provide meeting space, coffee, and staff the meetings with their leadership. These actions are welcomed by those in recovery, and often result in an increase in parish participation and membership.

One local church, which is across the street from the alternative high school, has "adopted" the students, offering food and adult interaction with the students. New relationships have been formed, with parishioners gaining a new understanding and awareness of teenage life and culture and the difficulties many students have in their lives. Hunger, homelessness, and students struggling with a variety of issues is now brought to life for those in the church who have connected with the school.

And, the school has greatly benefitted from involving their neighbors, and making those personal connections. Community service work flows both ways across the street.

Churches also participate the local Faith In Action program of Wellspring, providing respite "day care" for homebound people and their caregivers. Church members working in the program see real social issues up close and personal, and make personal connections, enriching everyone's lives by providing a meal, a safe place, and activities designed to stimulate and socialize those in extended care.

A number of churches host "Grub Club", a summer meal program for kids. Volunteers make lunches, which are handed out for free to kids during the summer. Food scarcity for kids is a major social crisis, and peaks during the summer when school (and the school cafeterias) are closed. Food comes from donations, the food bank and pantries, and some government funding. Many kids are "home alone" and often lack for food during the day, while their parents are working, and come to churches, schools, and libraries for a mid-day meal and some social interaction with other kids and adults. Libraries connect the kids with the summer reading program, and many kids take home a book.

My country western and rock guitar band meets every Thursday night in the basement of a local church. The church generously provides us with a warm room and a copy machine so we can share our music among ourselves. Often, the tables are filled with the latest church community project, including assembling school supplies, food, and warm clothing. It's a small church, but the tables are often full of items, and there are boxes and cupboards full of needed items, being assembled in order to be given away to those in need.

On any night of the week, there is a community supper available at a church in town, open to those in need of a meal and, during the rainy season, a warm place. There's some social outreach and companionship.

On cold nights, homeless folks can go to the warming center, staffed by volunteers, with cots, warm blankets, and some food. It is funded by local churches and charities and is open to anyone in need.

Another revolution has occurred in the last few years in our community. "Helping Hands" came to town and moved into an empty administration building left over from a World War II blimp base. The building was in disrepair and on its way to being razed. Yet, Helping Hands saw a need in the community for a transition space for those getting out of the local jail and state prisons. There is very limited transitional housing and a severe lack of programs for those finishing up their sentences and trying to re-establish their lives.

"Helping Hands" provides that, with decent housing and meals, rooms for families, and locating offices of needed social services, all in the same building. Transportation to other agencies and employment is provided, with a residential staff person developing plans and directing the residents to move forward on their plans. Local churches provide a variety of support and a small army of volunteers to move the program along.

The goal is to improve transitions and reduce the revolving door back to jail. The success is anecdotal and amazing. Not only are the clients helped, but everyone else who is involved has a warm heart and a sense of satisfaction of time and energy well spent.

In early winter, churches and other service organizations organize a "Homeless Connect" event for the local homeless population. The weather has turned cold and wet, yet many people are still living outside, sometimes literally "under the bridge". Forest campgrounds often are the homesites for people, who live in makeshift tents or cars. The luckier ones have adults and often kids in RVs that have seen better days.

"Homeless Connect" brings all the social service agencies together. A local church gym is taken over, and a hot meal is prepared. People can obtain health care, and connect with the employment office, food stamps, food pantries, and a wide range of clothing, including shoes and coats. Everyone can get a sleeping bag and a tent, yet those supplies run out fast. A local veterinarian provides free vaccinations and care for pets.

The response to that event is heart-wrenching and profound. People literally come out of the woods and are welcomed and helped. Help is provided, without the stigma and challenge of going to all the government offices spread around the community. There is dignity and generosity.

One of the privileges of volunteering in the community is being a witness to generosity. I was able to experience that event first-hand.

96

15 A DAY OF KINDNESS

I had a big dose of soul medicine and human kindness last week. The experience restored my faith in humanity and the power of unconditional love. I saw my community at its best.

A friend invited me to *Homeless Connect*, a community effort to provide basic needs to those among us who find themselves without shelter and other necessities.

The weather was bitter. Cold winds blew and temperatures were in the 20s at night. It wasn't so rough that the local warming shelter would be open, but it was still promising to be a miserable night.

My task was to be the greeter and the poll taker as folks left.

"Did you get what you needed?" and "What could we do better?"

I met a steady stream of people, people of all ages and circumstances. I didn't know their stories, and that kind of personal information was thankfully unwanted. We simply welcomed everyone who showed up and took care of basic needs. The red tape of bureaucracy was nowhere to be found. We did keep track of how many people came, as those without shelter are nearly invisible in our culture.

I saw a lot of smiles. Their pets were cared for, vaccinated, and fed. They had a hot meal and haircuts, were tended by health care providers, and connected with services by nearly every social service agency in town. They could pick up clean, warm clothes, blankets, sleeping bags, shoes, coats, tarps, and tents.

They made connections, not just with people and agencies who could offer a helping hand, but also with each other.

I saw connections made and strengthened with friends, family, an abundance of job prospects and housing tips. There was a spirit of fellowship and camaraderie filling the church gym where we had all gathered.

People were helping people, giving a helping hand, a ride, ideas and where to get help for a particular problem, connecting with others who cared. There was dignity and love.

It was an afternoon of suspended judgement and the absence of loudly voiced opinions and political rhetoric, blaming and stereotyping. Instead, it was a time of getting the right size of winter coat, a sleeping bag, a bag of food for someone's dog, a haircut, a hot meal, and a tip on a decent, safe place to pitch a tent.

Everyone helped everyone else. No one left without something to help them take better care of themselves, make their lives a little easier, and a feeling that they were an important part of the community.

Community. That was the unpublished message of the day. People had generously donated the food, clothing, bedding, pet care, medical care, and an afternoon of services to reach out to and help their fellow community members.

There were great conversations, interactions on problem solving and connecting people to each other, sharing resources and knowledge, being human and acting with kindness and compassion. There was respect.

The sun moved lower and the cold wind off the mountains pushed deeper through my coat, reminding me that night was coming. The people I was talking with were slowly drifting away, off to spend this night sleeping on the ground, with maybe only a tarp, a tent, and a sleeping bag to ward off the frosty air, and the loneliness of yet another night without permanent shelter.

I struggled to relate, to comprehend their lives.

I knew that I had a warm home to return to when my volunteer shift came to an end. There would be family to greet me, a hot meal on the stove, a comfortable chair, a good book, a warm, clean bed, and a bathroom with hot water and clean towels. I would not have to move on when the sun came up, putting all of my possessions into a plastic garbage bag, and maybe a backpack, and wondering where my next meal was coming from.

At home would be my assumptions about life, about meeting a person's basic needs and how people live in our community.

I assume a lot, yet I'm complacent, ignorant about how so many people in our community live, what they don't have, and what they can expect in the days to come. I find myself too often acting blind to the dilemma of such need in a society where some are wealthy, and there is an abundance of necessities, yet out of reach of so many.

For that afternoon at least, there was compassion, service, charity, and a common fellowship of people helping each other, of making lives more comfortable, more bearable. Another cold winter's night was coming, and dedicated community members had made a small effort to help ease people's circumstances, maybe helping them step forward into better times.

I learned, again, that in our humanity, it is not difficult to act with kindness and compassion. If I suspend judgement and comparison, if I try to walk a mile in another's shoes, then I can look at the world with greater understanding.

And, I can renew myself, and again be connected to the true purpose of our lives.

What is the impact of living one's faith and spiritual values in a community? What happens when you really get involved, step out of your comfort zone, and meet people where they are, and offer them a helping hand?

You change lives, you change yourself, and you change the community.

16 --- JUST LISTENING

"Listen with curiosity. Speak with honesty. Act with integrity. The greatest problem with communication is we don't listen to understand. We listen to reply. When we listen with curiosity, we don't listen with the intent to reply. We listen for what's behind the words." — Roy T. Bennett, *The Light in the Heart*

If we are committed to building community, one of the essential tools in our toolbox, an elemental aspect of our personality, is the skill of active listening. Roy Bennett, Stephen Covey and other commentators of the social scene, opine that we can't wait for the other person to stop talking so we can verbalize our own thoughts, our own selective and great wisdom.

In doing so, we minimize the other speakers' ideas and feelings, as we are so busy in our minds formulating our words, so we can return to center stage and speak our mind. If everyone is doing that, then there really isn't any conversation, just a series of monologs with a deaf audience.

A friend invited me to coffee, saying he needed my advice. We found a quiet corner in a café. There was chitchat, and he was fidgeting and starting to sweat.

"It's OK," I said. "It's just me. What's going on?"

He took a deep breath, looked up at the ceiling and out the window, then eyeballed his hands, clenched together around his coffee mug.

"It's my son," he began, letting out a whoosh of air.

I sat there, calm on the outside, a hand on my coffee mug. I tried to look open, inviting, and safe.

The story came pouring out, a tale of the teenaged son hiding out in his room, not coming out for dinner, not even any music playing or strumming on his guitar.

Dad got concerned and knocked on the door. There was no response, so he turned the knob and went in. The room was dark, with only a night light on. The son was sitting up on his bed, the dad's pistol in his lap and a hand wrapped around it.

The son was weeping and sniffling, not even looking up to acknowledge that dad was now in the room. Dad shut the door and sat next to the son, pretending to be calm, soothing, and unexcited. Inside, Dad's heart was pounding, he started to sweat, and his stomach turned over at what he was seeing.

Dad sat on the bed next to his son, not saying a word, just being there. Time seemed to stop, as Dad's mind raced through the options he had, wondering what words could be said. If he moved quickly to take the gun, the son's hand might find the trigger and fire the gun.

Dad took a breath, remembering the workshop he'd attended a number of months ago, when he was worried about a co-worker, and their talk about suicide and hopelessness. Dad had felt powerless.

"What can I do?" he had asked. Another co-worker referred him to the QPR program, and he signed up for a training in the community. QPR means "question, persuade, refer", and is a nationally recognized program to empower people to be gatekeepers, to have the skills and confidence to take action when you fear that someone close to you has suicidal thoughts. You're not a counselor, or a specialist, but you are given (and rehearse) tools to administer a form of first aid.

"The QPR mission is to reduce suicidal behaviors and save lives by providing innovative, practical and proven suicide prevention training. The signs of crisis are all around us. We believe that quality education empowers all people, regardless of their background, to make a positive difference in the life of someone they know."
https://qprinstitute.com

"QPR can be learned in our Gatekeeper course in as little as one hour.

"What is a Gatekeeper?

"According to the Surgeon General's National Strategy for Suicide Prevention (2001), a gatekeeper is someone in a position to recognize a crisis and the warning signs that someone may be contemplating suicide.

"Gatekeepers can be anyone, but include parents, friends, neighbors, teachers, ministers, doctors, nurses, office supervisors, squad leaders, foremen, police officers, advisors, caseworkers, firefighters, and many others who are strategically positioned to recognize and refer someone at risk of suicide."
https://qprinstitute.com

My friend and his son started to talk. Dad was careful to not be judgmental or condemning. He asked open ended questions and opened the door for some serious, deep conversation about his son's life, his feelings, and choices that he had.

Dad knew that if he tried to quickly grab the gun or make a sudden move, his son might unintentionally fire the pistol, or decide to take the next step in his suicide plan. Dad kept calming himself down and continue the gentle, quiet conversation. Time was on his side, and also his son's.

Dad's patience paid off and the son finally said he was ready for his dad to take the pistol. They talked about where to go from here, with Dad suggesting a counselor at the local mental health clinic. He'd heard good things about them, and so had the son.

"I can go with you, if you want, son. I love you and I support you. I want the best for you."

The son cried some more and put his arms around his dad. Dad cried, too, embracing his son and expressing his love.

My friend wept as he told me this story. We'd both taken that workshop together, and I kept my little pamphlet, with the outline of questions and helpful statements, and the national suicide hotline number, in my backpack. I'd had a few occasions to refer to it, when people approached me and said they needed help.

I took him out for lunch a few weeks later and didn't want to pry about his son. We talked about other things in our life. He brought up his son, and said he's doing better now, seeing the counselor and changing some of his routine at school. He's taken up a new hobby and is looking for a few new friends.

My friend said they've started a new habit, going out to breakfast on Saturday morning, just him and his son. There's no agenda, and no expectations. They just have a good time and catch up on the week's activities. Sometimes, the son talks about his feelings, and sometimes not. But the door is open, and Dad thinks his son realizes that his door is always open to him, and they can talk about anything.

One time, I was walking into the grocery store, and a friend was sitting on the bench outside, staring into his hands, looking pale and downtrodden. I decided my grocery list could wait and I sat next to him, just sitting there. Soon, he started talking, telling me of his illness, and how he wasn't able to work anymore. He was getting some help, but some days were harder than others. Coming to the grocery store was a big deal for him, as crowds of people could set him off, raising his level of anxiety to an intolerable level.

"Thanks for caring about me," he said. "I'm alright. Life just overwhelms me sometimes."

Rural communities are small, and there are few secrets. There's gossip but there's also a great deal of concern and affection for our families, friends, and neighbors. We rub shoulders a lot with each other in our daily lives, but we seldom take the time to really answer the question "How are you doing?"

The socially correct answer is "fine and, how are you?" But "fine" is not always the honest, the correct answer. Sometimes, the answer is a great deal more complex and emotionally charged.

Good friends dig in, hit the "pause" button, and ask a few more questions. There's trust and confidence, knowing that the answer won't be blabbed about to other friends or neighbors, or be posted on social media.

Real friends probe deeper, if the signs are there. Health issues, emotional crises, unhealthy relationships are all held close to the vest by most of us. We don't want to be embarrassed, or reveal "too much", or have an awkward conversation about something that is personal and private. Yet, we know that a "good ear", a quiet and non-judgmental friend is hopefully close by.

"I don't want to be a bother," would be what my aunt would say, as she would lament not letting people know what was really going on in her life. Being a loving relative or a good friend is about being bothered, though. Bother me, because I care about you. Let me in on your secrets, so you can hear yourself give voice to your worries and woes. By hearing what is going on with you inside, then you can process the worry, and begin to make sense of it, do some problem solving, and figure out an action plan.

When you do that with a friend, you deepen the friendship, you deepen the trust. Life becomes less burdensome, and your soul becomes lighter. Life looks rosier, or at lease more manageable.

We live in a well-connected world, our phones providing an almost unlimited gateway to people, facts, and activities. Our thoughts, opinions, photos, and activities find a ready audience to literally hundreds, if not thousands of people. Those of us who use social media to snoop on others find a treasure house of details and information our grandparents would find embarrassing, and compelling evidence of narcissistic pride and conceit. Perhaps the legend of Narcissus today would be told with a smart phone in her hand.

There are a lot of churches in our communities, busy on Sunday mornings and Wednesday evenings. There are a lot of activities, centered around spirituality and the common gathering of those sharing the same faith. Ministers are busy tending to the needs of their congregations and offer a sanctuary and advice for many of the burdens that people carry. Religion can offer answers and solutions, and a community of healing and forgiveness.

Healing can occur anywhere.

There are other churches in town, other confessionals and places of fellowship, communion and blessing. The line at the grocery store, the back table at the coffee shop, the kitchen table or the front porch, or a few minutes at a community event. Sometimes, the work is done during a break at work, or a meal with a friend you haven't seen for a while. In these places, important work is done. The work, the ministry of listening, of setting aside your own "to do list", and your own agenda, and sit quietly.

Like my friend and his son, in the midst of a suicidal crisis, the instrument of harm at hand, and there is space given, an opening. Time stops, and the "pause button" in our lives is hit. Everything else takes a back seat, and the most important thing to do, the most important action step, is to listen. Listen with compassion, seeking understanding and relationship. The fruits of such work are abundant.

17 --- WANTING CHANGE: HOW DOES THAT HAPPEN??

Often, I react to the news with despair, anger and frustration. I remind myself that the "news" is often sensationalized, that the news business is a business, and that almost all the "good news" is not included in a news program. Yet, what much of what is "news" stirs me up to wanting change, a different approach to old problems.

If I want change, I have to act.

If I am passive, then others will make changes, or not. And those actions or inactions will likely not be what I want to see happen. I will not have a voice. My silence, my inaction diminishes my soul and my purpose in life.

"You must be the change you want to see in the world," Mahatma Gandhi famously said.

Yet, to borrow a phrase from Al Gore, it is an inconvenient truth.

If I don't like what I read in the news, then either I am an instrument to change the world, or I do nothing. My inaction assures that I lose my right to express my disagreement with what is going on. After all, actions speak louder than words.

I am in charge of how I react, respond, how I am an instrument of change, putting action into my beliefs, and thus creating change, building a better world.

If I don't like what I see in my community, my neighborhood, my family, then I need to step up and get involved, and become an instrument of change.

A healthier community starts with me. Put up or shut up. It's all on me.

The simple acts are the easiest and the most effective. They have the greatest impact long term.

Here's a list of actions for me, and, hopefully, you:

- Invite a friend to coffee.
- Play music, and teach someone else, sharing music with others, creating joy and community.
- Start a conversation with a stranger.
- Send an inspirational note or story to a friend.
- Reach out to a prisoner, someone who is going through a hard patch, someone in pain.
- Acknowledge someone's loss, or a challenge, and offer them a compliment, a few words of cheer and encouragement. They are not alone.
- Practice patience and understanding.
- Don't expect a reward or recognition. Acting anonymously can be very sweet. It can become contagious.
- Practice forgiveness and compassion, even if another's words or acts seem hurtful.
- Imagine walking in the shoes of another.
- Remember the Greek proverb: "A society grows great when old men plant trees whose shade they shall never sit in."
- Slow to judge, quicker to forgive.
- Intend to follow the Golden Rule.
- Examine your own biases and prejudices. Do some personal housekeeping. I've found this to be very humbling and enlightening.
- Suspend judgement.
- Don't assume.

My ego gets in the way in this work, but if I am honest, I learn more about myself and the world, and I move forward to be a better human being.

And, the world changes, just a little.

18 --- BEATEN

Domestic violence and childhood trauma are epidemics in our communities. Bessel van der Kolk's book, *The Body Keeps the Score: Brain, Mind, and Body in the Healing of Trauma,* is compelling, insightful and essential reading for the builders of community.

My friend Tristan speaks to the very essence.

Beaten

Where will you place it

this time

There isn't much space

on my skin that hasn't

been marked by your fury

Even less room remains on

my heart for another scar

Your eyes are wild with hate

Unprovoked anger spins from

your tongue

My eyes are blank and tearless

They've run themselves dry

I feel unworthy so I stay

Expecting, accepting another blow

Your soul is black

For some unknown reason

Something has hurt you

so you hurt me

Hurt hung onto too long manifests

itself into anger

You try to transfer it to me

but it still resides in you

So where will you place

it this time

When my skin has turned

to ash…

---- Tristan ©2017

19 --- SUPPORTING OTHERS

Good and unexpected things happen when you are out running an errand.

It was a mundane trip to the bank, getting change for an upcoming community dinner and musical event. I was the cashier, so I needed to make change. There were other things on my list, and I was checking them off. The bank errand was one of the least exciting.

On my way in from the parking lot, a man called out to me, wanting to say "hi". I hadn't seen him around town for a while, but he wanted to talk. In a small town, it is all about relationships, and being "on time" isn't very important.

I've learned always to stop and talk. It is the polite thing to do, it is building and maintaining community, and sometimes, it saves a life.

He told me that he's clean and sober now, but a month ago, he tried to kill himself. A double dose of heroin on a cold, wet riverbank, just wanting to end his pain.

He didn't die and he had a long talk with God in the darkest part of the night, and the darkest moments of his life.

"You're at your most honest, most naked, when it is completely dark outside, you've just tried to kill yourself and the only one around to talk to is God," he said.

"I decided to live. God has things for me to do."

He didn't elaborate; no details were forthcoming. His message about life and purpose and recover was short and direct.

We'd always been honest with each other. He was a defendant in court sometimes and I was the judge. We had different roles and different perspectives. Our different missions and purposes crossed paths once in a while, but we saw eye to eye more than we disagreed.

In those times, he kept on getting high and drunk and being violent, and I kept trying to hold him accountable, imposing penalties and punishments and ignored advice on being a good citizen and loving himself. It was an odd friendship, but we had some good, heart to heart talks, and often agreed to disagree, given the roles we had in the courtroom.

Eventually, there was progress, reform, moving forward to a life of occasional penance and sobriety, reformation along the twelve-step path.

These days, I stay out of the courtroom and so does he. I see his Facebook posts and on occasion, I see him around town. For my friend, it is one day at a time. I admire his courage, his determination.

He's honest about who he is, and where he's at.

I really have no true sense of the demons he wrestles with in his life, and I see him being brave and determined in his journey. With what he's shared with me and on social media, I think the demons are humongous and treacherous. People of lesser courage and guts would have given up, thrown in the towel. He hasn't. He keeps going, one step at a time, one day at a time.

There are stumbles and setbacks; understandable given the magnitude of what he is dealing with inside of him.

Today, we meet at the door of the bank, catching up. He's alive, sober, and moving ahead in his life. That's today's good news, and I'm grateful for our friendship.

I see another man in the bank, a high school classmate. He's back in town now, after many years of working in the city. He's a high school coach, on his way to his team's first game in the state playoffs.

He's grinning ear to ear, attired in the high school colors and wearing the team's sweats and cap.

"I'm loving what I'm doing, coaching kids, giving back to the community," he says.

On my way out, on the sidewalk, another man stops me to say hi. He's familiar, but his name escapes me. I know him to be a veteran from Afghanistan, troubled by PTSD, drugs and alcohol. We've had good talks too, in the roles we played in the courtroom. His war terrors brought him an anguished life coping with strained relationships, trying to parent kids, trying to stay employed and stable.

There have been binges and relapses, recovery, reconciliation and more nightmares, more police calls, a few suicide attempts. Getting arrested, some jail time, and probation-mandated treatment haven't been the panacea to break the cycle, yet he keeps trying.

We've had conversations, formal and informal, the best ones over coffee after running into each other in a cafe. When all else has failed, he's tried honesty and reformation, trying new ways to change his life, and take on his anger and rage.

His stubbornness and pride have kept him from being frank with a counselor and taking on his demons. I've learned that real change doesn't start until one has reached the proverbial bottom, and he's finally gotten there.

A good friend took him to the VA and he found a counselor who could speak the same language. They connected, got down and dirty, and he was able to wrestle with his dragons and find his sword.

There was support in the community, including the police officer who'd been to his house too many times, who'd hooked him up and transported him to jail, and escorted him to court enough times that they were on a first name basis.

He got connected to AA and NA in town and was able to see the light and a way out of his nightmares. There were familiar faces in the groups, and similar stories. These meetings are confidential and supportive. Peoples speak their truth and share their pain. They are embraced and loved, welcomed into the community.

When he was well down this path of meetings, counseling, sharing, and "finding his tribe", his name starting to go missing from the police log and the court dockets. He had new friends and started to smile and laugh sometimes.

I saw him one time.

"Can't talk long," he said. "I'll be late for work."

We both laughed. Being regularly employed was something new for him, and he was bursting with pride for having that new obligation, a new reason not to talk to the judge.

We shook hands, and I told him I was proud of him.

He beamed and laughed again and took his leave.

His probation officer wrote me a year after his last court appearance, asking that his probation be ended. He was doing everything he needed to do, and more. He was well on his journey of sobriety and redemption, and in need of forgiveness and being able to move on with his life.

He was now a strong, healthy member of the community.

An Anchor in a Storm

We are often called to stand by a friend, offering a hand and being their anchor.

A friend was recently in the middle of a storm in his life, a challenge that required his full concentration and talents. I knew he was up for the challenge, and had been preparing for it for some time, with a great deal of thought and energy. He was focused, zeroing in on what needed to be done, what was critical for success.

Yet, the task was daunting, overwhelming at times.

"I've never done this before," he confided in me. He voiced doubt, insecurity, talking of the old demons that walked through his life, and so many lives of people I know, including my own.

I'm good at doubting myself, finding pessimism and self-criticism in abundance. There's a lot of things I haven't done before either. Walking into new territory is perilous. I've failed, too, and have those recurring thoughts of worthlessness and inadequacy. The journey opens me up to be vulnerable and to risk failure and criticism. The worst critic is often me, and I can readily rattle off a long list of why I will fail at something. Others tell me I'm not alone in having that self judgement and self-sabotage. Friends can joke with me that such talents can be turned around, becoming our greatest strengths.

Sometimes, I'm the storm-tossed boat and sometimes I am the anchor for someone else. Life is like that, taking turns with others, being on each other's journeys, a hand reaching out to another hand.

With my friend, I sensed a need to step forward and be an anchor. I invited myself along in his task, volunteering to be the listener to a long litany of doubt and fear, the one who waits while he took on his challenging task. It took almost everything he had to meet his challenge, and he had to do it alone.

I held space for him, being nearby, prepared to give both comfort and encouragement. The nature of the challenge didn't allow us to communicate, but in important ways, we did. He knew I was there, being supportive, being present, being the vessel of his hopes and dreams, fears and doubts. I accepted all of that, absorbing the bad, reflecting the good of who he was and what he was experiencing.

When the Herculean task was done, I was the giver of hugs, the cheerleader, the repository of his relief and his doubts that they had done a good job. I encouraged, I empathized. I was the listener in chief.

Afterwards, I took him to dinner and. He could barely get in the truck and buckle his seatbelt. His sentences were just fragments, a serious case of being "brain dead".

I made sure that he could look out into nature as he ate and began to process the day's experience, unwinding and coming into the normal world, able to breathe in the beauty of this day.

I recalled other "anchoring" duties, many of them in the arena of hospitals and bedsides; the stark and cold visiting areas in jails and outside courtrooms; the midnight talks when there seemed to be no hope, no direction into the future. There was the time I sat in a darkened room, the pistol cocked and loaded in my buddy's lap, clenched in his fist, as he cried out the tragedy of his life. The time my aunt was my anchor, inviting me over to tea but really calling me to task, taking me into a profound conversation about life and my future.

Anchoring changes lives and saves lives. There's magic, because one often doesn't know what really works to help give that essential support and love.

When duty calls, you show up and you become the anchor, the rock, and hopefully the healer. The work is a gift from the heart. When your own storm is raging, you remember you need your own anchor, and you reach out to someone who cares. Then, you truly realize the power of this gift.

We are called, as humans, to hold space for others, to be their anchor in the storms that buffet their lives. We need to be a witness, a presence in their lives, so that they are not alone, they can know that they matter to others, that their struggles are honored, their journeys worthwhile.

21 NAVIGATING RELATIONSHIPS

Navigating the challenging seas of relationships is a big part of community. For me, being in community is going from the inside out. I have to be in touch with myself, and then my family, and then, if that is in order, I can help with and work in my community.

"Community is a group of individuals who have learned how to communicate honestly with each other, whose relationships go deeper than their masks of composure, and who have developed some significant commitment to 'rejoice together, mourn together'', and to 'delight in each other, make others' condition our own'. " — M. Scott Peck, *The Different Drum*

Several of my friends are counselors, working in the tough fields of marriage, relationships, parenting, addiction, and the changes in life we are all faced with.

They are the tradesmen of human relationships, who help us get our personal and domestic houses in order, by mending what is broken, or building an additional skill or insight, of making things work better.

An especially wise counselor told me that if I didn't care so much about my partner, it wouldn't be so hard to communicate, and to work through a problem. To make it easy, I could just walk away. Being in love makes us stubborn, and we desperately want our relationships to work, because we care.

A young man I know recently broke up with his girlfriend. His heart was broken, and he knew he had to move on. Yet, the pain was still there, and he needed to mourn and lick his wounds.

He's smart and insightful enough to know that he needed some time to himself. He also needed to talk about it and speak out loud of his pain and the ways that helped him really feel his emotions, not covering them up or stuffing them down deep inside of himself.

It was painful to hear, the sniffling and loneliness, the ache of his heart. We've all been there, and my empathy brought my own heart to ache.

We commiserated, and I tried to avoid the platitudes and the insensitive remarks and commentary.

"Oh, you'll get over it."

"There's other fish in the sea."

"She wasn't the right one for you. It's good you found that out early on."

All those remarks do is make you feel foolish you even met her, let alone fell in love. You obviously can't be making good choices about love yet.

And, the ultimate cut to the bone, "You're so stupid."

How do we help out fellow humans when Cupid's arrow seems to have been misfired, and two people aren't in love with each other anymore, or at least when one of you decides they are done, leaving the other to wonder why and to mourn a tragic loss?

As a builder of community, how do I try to give some first aid, and help my friend start to heal.

My first rule is to not gossip about it. Respect their confiding in me, their privacy. When you hear those tales of woe, you are the priest in the confessional, and I need to listen with respect and decency.

Just letting my friend vent and weep can be more than enough to help them. You give them space to say their words, so that it becomes a reality, something that is actually there.

We are, after all, healers of the community woes, and helping to heal broken hearts makes for healthy people who can then come back into the community ready to engage in the world and be emotionally healthy.

Here's what I wrote to my friend, after our deep conversation over the phone:

Dear Jim:

Here are some of my thoughts about relationships and love.

Oh, thinking about love, and romance and commitment, relationship, dating, and awkward. Especially the awkward. Then, there's the old nemesis: rejection, abandonment, breaking up. There's no good word for that. And, we don't know how to talk about all that very well.

There's too much pain, too much self-doubt, agony, and being open to dealing with what my more fearful self calls "not good enough", being a screw up, a failure, and simply no good at navigating love and relationship.

At my age, you think I'd be an expert now. I'm certainly experienced. But, not top of the line knowledgeable, not proficient, certainly not comfortable with dealing with my emotions, let alone easily and expertly consoling a friend who has recently escaped from the battlefield, with bleeding wounds, and armor in disarray.

I'm really vulnerable to issues involving my heart and my sensitivity and my desire to be a loving, sweet, and kind person. Old scars and old wounds are still around, and the old demons, and the old ways are easily resurrected, and rearmed. I've worked hard at trying to put old ways, old experiences, and old responses behind me, and to move on. I've spent a lifetime learning to be healthy, to practice self-care, and fresh, clean ways of thinking and processing, and navigating through life.

Yet, it doesn't take much to stir things up inside of me again, raising old nasty emotions and thinking and attitudes. I've learned from most of my mistakes and gained personal insight and tools on how to be a better, more loving and lovable man. Still, I'm vulnerable, and the armor I still wear isn't always effective in deflecting the arrows and spears that a person can throw at me. I can get off the rails pretty easily.

I am who I am, warts and defects and flaws still intact. So, world, be gentle on me, be kind, and love me for who I am.

We all have flaws. And, flaws in a diamond or a pearl only add to their beauty. Perfect is boring and doesn't make for a better lover, a gentler, kinder soul.

I still find people who will happily rummage through my own closet of unfun memories and nightmares, and shove those events in my face, reminding me that I screwed up, that I blew it, and that I was less than ideal and perfect. And, to what end? To make themselves feel more superior, better than me, and to throw me in the gutter of despair and self-loathing?

I really don't need that in my life, and I try to be conscious about keeping those mean-spirited people a safe distance from me. I'm really better than that, and I don't deserve it. None of us do. This is self-care work and needs to be done often.

And, I don't build up my life by putting others down. I do better when we all get lifted up by each other, support each other, and help each other be better lovers of ourselves and others.

I have certain expectations in a relationship. And, a lot of that is non-negotiable. Here's my list of what I need and what I expect:

- Respect. No put downs, no degrading, no telling others bad stories about me, and painful stuff from my past. I may share those, so you can understand me better, and how I think and react and behave. But my past is MY story, to be shared only by me under my terms. I'm a private person and I don't share my past and my wounds easily. It's treacherous territory and I can easily feel vulnerable and afraid. When I feel that way, I can lash out and be a mean tiger in the jungle. Don't go there with me. It's not pretty.
- Encouragement. Life is challenging, and I'm not always successful or skilled in navigating through it. Sometimes, I am overwhelmed or not able to quickly find my path today. I need your support, your encouragement, your belief in me

that this too shall pass, and we can move on. Your support doesn't always have to be verbal, but I do need to know you are at my side, and that you believe in my ultimate goodness.

- Reciprocity. What I expect from you is what you should expect from me. A relationship is a partnership, a team, and we are both expected to give 100% to us. It's not 50/50, it's not half and half, or "if I feel like it" or "if it is convenient". Crisis and need come at inconvenient times, and I need you to be here for me when I need it. And, the same for you.

- Commitment. In thick and thin, better or worse, richer or poorer. Those words are in wedding vows for a reason.

- Communication. I am lousy at reading minds, and little better in being intuitive and sensitive. I do so much better when you can share your pain, your doubts, your worries, your needs. The elephant often lives in the living room and the bedroom, but we need to acknowledge its presence and its impact on our lives. Then, we can deal with it.

- Skill. We are skilled at life, and experienced. Together, we can sharpen our tools and find the right tools, and work through the problem, the issue, and communicate with each other. If you think I'm a screw up, I am at least a skilled screw up and this isn't my first rodeo.

- Love. The word is often over-used and can get worn out. But it is what I really want and need. You do too. I think it is my primary goal in life, and my primary driving force and need. And, hate is not the opposite. The real opposite word is indifference. Don't be indifferent with me, taking me for granted, or using me as a doormat. I respond to love, and hopefully my responses add beauty to the world. Not loving me evokes a different response, and I don't want that, and I will leave, in search of true love.

- Integrity. Both my partner and I having integrity, morality, decency, and compassion towards others.

- Partnership. One of my primary tasks is to help my partner grow in their life, their creativity, their capacity for being loving, to be loved, and to love others. To help them achieve their passion and their possibilities. When they grow, I benefit, and I then also have the capacity to grow. We grow each other. We enhance each other, we support each other, in every way. We are a team. We protect each other and we look out for each other. We ease the bumps in the road, and we are open to opening up possibilities for the other. We are gardeners for each other.

-

Life can be painful and confusing, and I sometimes lose my way. A loving partner sometimes takes the wheel, and guides me to my quiet, peaceful place, and loves me.

Communities need to talk about these feelings and these challenges, too. Communities go through their challenges, their fights, their "marital woes", as the fabric of our lives sometimes becomes frayed and needing some repairs and tender loving care.

Perhaps if we looked at community life as a form of marriage, we would be a little more tender and kinder, more forgiving, and willing to sit down over a cup of coffee, admit we made some mistakes, and say that we are sorry. We really do love each other, so how do we make it better?

21 --- STRUGGLING WITH LONELINESS

I see a lot of loneliness in our society. Ironically, it is everywhere, and often found in the busiest places of our communities. With all of our personal technology, and seemingly effortless tools to "keep in touch", we struggle with an epidemic of isolation. Loneliness is often invisible, seldom talked about, and not an easy topic of conversation. There's a social taboo on vocalizing our emotional states, anyway, and falling silent and withdrawing is one of the traits of the lonely and isolated.

Three quarters of Americans have experienced moderate to acute loneliness. And, a quarter of us are at the high end of that emotional range. US News and World Report

Loneliness is most prevalent in ages under 25 and over 65.

I recently came upon a friend, sitting by himself, head in his hands, in the middle of the busiest part of a big store.

Instead of tending to my shopping list and a busy day, I sat with him, and honored the silence between us. He looked up, barely acknowledging me, and then resumed staring at his hands and the floor. He's normally talkative with me, telling stories of his kids, his work, and his art. Now, just silence, and a lot of pain. I felt his loneliness in the air we breathed, and from the bench where we sat.

My friend isn't usually like this, brooding and silent. There's something deep going on, I thought, and I best take the time to just be here with my friend.

The silence deepened, but it felt comfortable. I could tell that my presence was welcome, and that I should stay.

People whirled around us, the noise of shopping carts and kids, lots of conversations filling up the space. My friend's silence became even more noteworthy in all the chaos and tumult. Intuitively, I decided to stay, my friend needing someone to just be with. Just being present is a valuable and often greatly appreciated act of friendship.

My friend took a deep breath and sighed, and then began to talk, his voice barely above a whisper. He told a tale of anxiety and despair, how life has been a struggle, and that no one cared about him.

"I care," I said.

"I know," he replied. He talked more, the emotional dam letting loose, dark thoughts and pent up feelings spilling out, filling up the comfortable silence that we had. He looked me in the eye and told a funny story on himself.

We laughed and he said he felt better, just being able to talk about life with someone.

"I'm better now," he said. "You don't have to worry about me now. I'll be alright."

"And thanks," he said. "Thanks for sitting with me and being my friend."

A few years ago, I took an empowering training on being sensitive to depression and suicidal ideation, QPR Training. That experience gave me the confidence to tune up my intuition and my compassion and be able to be of some help to those in need of help in dark times. I asked a few questions, and said I knew of some resources if he needed them. He said he wasn't at risk, but he appreciated my concern and the offer. He thanked me for being a friend, and for taking the time to care.

Isn't that task in the job description of being a human being and living in society? We all need to be aware and to take the time to help a fellow human being.

The rest of the day, I was more aware of the loneliness around me, and in my community. I made it a point to talk to people in the store, and say "hi", how are you doing?", and really meaning it.

The checkout clerk and I had a good conversation, and I realized that even though she was inundated with customers throughout her shift, the work can be lonely and isolating.

"There's a misperception that loneliness means social isolation," Dr. Dilip Jeste, a professor of psychiatry and neuroscience at the University of California at San Diego, said. "Loneliness is subjective. It is what you feel. The definition of loneliness is distress because of a discrepancy between actual social relationships and desired social relationships. There's a discrepancy between what I want and what I have."

Like most of us, I experience loneliness and depression. Those emotions are part of my humanity, and likely are at least partly influenced by the turmoil and pressures of our society, which corrode my efforts to take care of myself and be healthy. I've tried to build into my self-care regimen some tools to be less lonely, more connected with others. Among those tools are exercise, nutrition, taking time to be in nature, creativity, and engaging with others.

Volunteerism is suggested by Dr. Kasley Killam, in her article, *A Solution for Loneliness*, in the May 2019 edition of *Psychology Today*. She urges us to volunteer at least two hours a week, which can reduce our sense of loss of meaning, and reverse cognitive decline. 2/3 of volunteers reported they now felt less isolated, which addresses the fact that a fourth to half of all Americans feel lonely a lot of the time. Loneliness makes many of us more prone to developing a wide range of physical and mental illnesses, including heart disease, cancer, diabetes and depression.

Self-care and community care, they go hand in hand and make a better world for all of us.

22 --- BEING PRESENT IN THE LIVES OF OTHERS

Being Present

is often the greatest gift, the

highest act of friendship.

No expectation of conversation,

yet the richest communication

(communing --- action).

The most difficult, the most awkward

the most challenging

is simply to just be

be in the lives of another

suspending opinion, commentary,

judgement. Breathing in the quiet.

Saying it all, without voice.

In the quiet, much is conveyed

and what is hard becomes

eased, relaxed, now flowing

back and forth

communicated.

Silence is love in action

an opening, a sharing

relational, transformative

soul changing.

I am present in the world, I am taking a step forward, in the right direction, focused.

What is leadership, service? Where are we headed? In the direction we are facing, where we are stepping into, away from where we have been – in the past and into the future.

If I want to change, I have to act.

If I am passive, then others will make change, or not. And I will not have a role, a voice in that change I want to see. Being passive diminishes my soul, and my purpose in life.

"You must be the change you want to see in the world." Mahatma Gandhi.

If I don't like what I read in the news, then either I am an instrument to change the world, or I do nothing. If I do nothing, then I lose my right to express my disagreement with what is going on.

If I don't like what I see in my community, then I need to step up and get involved, be an instrument of change. A healthier community starts with me.

Put up or shut up; it's all on me.

I am in charge of how I react and respond. How am I an instrument of change, putting action into my beliefs? If I create change then I must act and have the intention to build a better world.

The simple acts are the easiest and the most effective:

- Playing music and teaching someone else in sharing music in the community is one path.
- Starting a conversation with a stranger, inviting a friend to coffee, sending someone in need an inspirational note, or a meaningful story, can change a life.
- Reaching out to a prisoner, a shut-in, or someone who needs a hand getting their groceries into their car, can change a life and better a community.
- Paying kindness forward, practicing patience and understanding, and not expecting a reward or recognition. Practicing forgiveness and compassion, even if another's words or acts seem hurtful.
- Imagine walking in the shoes of another, and seeing the world, and the situation at hand from their eyes, can change your own perspective.
- Planting a tree, making a small part of the world more beautiful, without considering if you would profit from the act, are acts of change.
- Be slow to judge and quicker to forgive.
- Form the intention to follow the Golden Rule.
- Often, I gain insight into my own self when I look deep into my own biases and prejudices and do some personal housekeeping.
- Suspend judgment.

• Don't assume.

A Conversation Over Coffee

We hadn't met before, just an introduction from a friend, then a few e-mails, and wanting to get together. She was writing a book and thought I'd be a good interview subject for her. She wanted to pick my brain and get my perspective.

We lived 90 miles apart, and agreed to meet halfway, in a town we each didn't know all that well and have coffee. It took some effort, but we agreed on a coffee shop neither of us had been to and set a time.

I'd been interviewed before, but I'm always nervous about meeting a stranger, and having them ask me questions. I had the general topic, but really no idea of what she really wanted to know about me and my opinions on the topic.

It was an uncomfortable topic: addictions. I'm passionate about efforts to deal with addictions, treatment, and recovery, and also the darker question of what gets people into addictive behavior.

It is an uncomfortable subject, as I don't consider myself as an expert or someone who has a ready grasp of the answers.

I wondered why she wanted to interview me, and doubt crept in on whether I could be of any help in her research.

Addiction and I have a personal relationship and digging into it always raises discomfort and pain for me. There's been times in my life that alcohol did some awful things in my life and I distanced myself from it. I did that blindly and without guidance from people I trusted, while still living in a culture where drinking was the norm, and you needed to drink in order to fit in and be a real man. Or so I thought.

I have family and friends who have wrestled with addiction and abuse of alcohol and drugs. And, sometimes that relationship was incredibly destructive, and sometimes, fatal. The wrestling and struggles with addiction changes lives and relationships and creates barriers that are often insurmountable, or just incredibly difficult and strained. For many people I know, those battles continue.

In my work in the legal system, addiction was the dominant theme of nearly every case I worked on, and the responses and "remedies" of the legal system often seemed to me to be inadequate and ineffective. The fallback position was putting the person in jail or sending them to prison, with a Hail Mary prayer that times behind bars would solve the problem, get their attention, and answer the question of how we stop them from doing all that addiction-fired behavior again.

The lawyers and judges who I regarded with respect and expertise seemed to believe that, and one of the legal system's mantras is that prison rehabilitates people. And, popular political sentiment has been that the system should protect the innocent victims and society generally by incarcerating the "bad boys".

I'd always felt that the "success rating" in my work in the system, and on a personal level always ran the full range of success and failure. I kept testing hypotheses, talked to experts and addicts, friends and family. My approaches seemed rather piecemeal and experimental, and, as always, not given to tried and true remedies and successes.

There were certainly others who had more expertise, more "battlefield experience", who would be more engaging as an interview subject.

The writer showed up at the coffee shop a few minutes after me, and we settled in with coffee and sharing stories about our mutual friend, the one who had connected us, expressing the thought that "we had a lot in common".

She was experienced in the field of addiction recovery, working as a counselor, developing case management plans, overseeing treatment, and digging into the tough issues with addicts and families, using the professional methodologies she had learned in grad school and in her years of work in the field.

Her work and experience, much like mine, has let her conclude that addiction behavior is the result of unresolved and unrelieved trauma, trauma that was experienced in childhood. As well, trauma that has been carried from generation to generation to generation and is continuing to poison and limit people in being able to cope with life. People can find ways of being emotionally healthy without the self-medication of alcohol and drugs.

She wants to tell the stories of addiction, self-discovery, and treatment, in hopes of inspiring professionals as well as society generally that there is hope, and there are resources and skills we can all utilize to be healthier.

We found our commonalities, coming at the issues from two viewpoints, the counselor and the lawyer.

I told my stories, recalling successes and tragedies. She took notes, recharged her tape recorder, and kept asking for more stories, more reflection, more of the angst and emotional pain that reverberates inside of me as I keep talking.

We feel safe with each other, developing trust, and a common bond. We are helpers and healers, each with our tools, our compassion, our humanity.

I give her my book on my experiences with sitting with people, listening, caring, and sometimes, guiding them out of the wilderness. I imagine my book is full of hope, and she hopes the same for her book.

As we talk, part of me pulls back, taking a broader, more "forest for the trees" perspective, and I can see what we are doing. We are being present with each other, in the moment, fully engaged, listening with all of our senses and all of our heart. We care passionately about the subject and we are now caring passionately about this conversation.

We will both be changed by this conversation, our professional work and thoughts strengthened by knowing that the other person also deeply cares about the issues and has resources we could access. The other is also "working the problem" and finding better tools.

I put her in touch with a friend of mine, who has had a long, complicated relationship with addiction, devastating his family, going to jail, and coming close to death. Yet, he has changed, reformed, and re-emerged from the other end of the war zone profoundly changed. He's a leader in the sobriety movement and now is a full-time healer in the community.

His story is amazing and she is eager to connect with him and sit with him for an interview.

Our cup of coffee is like an intersection on a spider web, and more connections, more weavings and web buildings are the result of our conversation.

We realize we are both web builders, weavers on the loom of social interaction and community building. And, we laugh, sharing our observations and conclusions, and the joy of finding another kindred spirit.

When you realize you aren't working alone, that other people share your vision, use the same tools, and have the same interests in the community, the world expands for you, and becomes a richer, more vibrant, and healthy place.

The next week, she is interviewing my friend. They invite me over to his house, as she thinks there are gaps in the stories I told and the ones he told, about how we have interacted together. In a few minutes, she is interviewing both of us, laughing about how we interact with each other, enjoying our friendship.

She sees how he and I are weavers, too, and have taken on challenging projects, and touched the lives of many people. We have different tools, but we are both part of the team.

A few weeks later, she shares her writing of our meeting, asking for corrections and revisions. It is her story, not mine, in many ways, and I am hesitant to edit her personal observations. She has captured my passion and my worries for the community, and that is enough for me. I am satisfied with her work and with our experience.

I didn't have much invested in this experience; a couple hours of driving, a cup of coffee, some few hours of conversation about life experiences, and how I have thought about the people I've worked with, cried with, and connected with on very deep and intimate levels.

Part of a day, and then a few hours, when I got to see an old friend and share our passions, was all that I can say was a "commitment". Yet, it was a building project, feeding the souls of three people, and strengthening the weaving and community building that are so needed in every community.

I'm sure some other magical things occurred in that coffee shop that morning. Friendships were strengthened, perhaps a marriage revitalized, a problem with a child answered, a few business deals made. Or maybe everyone was talking about addiction and recovery. All those conversations were equally important.

Yet for me, the most important part of that experience was having the connection, having the tough conversation, and building relationships.

23 --- HOLDING SPACE

These are not gentle times. And, having a mean streak seems almost a requirement these days, as we navigate social media and the cultural and political climate.

Our culture, and so many commentators and "leaders", are so quick to make judgement, to express opinions, and eagerly offer criticism and condemnation of others' points of view. Political, social, and artistic criticism now is so often unkind, harsh, even vicious to the point of hostility and intolerance.

It is an easy train to climb aboard, and my snarky and off-handed comments are often a computer click away from getting out into the world, showing up on the social media "news feeds" that have become the path by which most of us engage with others. Be quick, spontaneous, "get it out there", and move on to something else. The popular term, "click bait" comes to mind as having a meaning larger than how we define the term. Is being polite too time consuming, too unfashionable? It seems easier just to fire off a salvo, and "let it fly".

We've come a long way from the days when social commentary and personal expression in public came after laboring over a sheet of linen paper with a quill pen, and a pot of ink. A letter to the editor not only took time to compose and hand write, but also required an envelope, a stamp, and a trip to the post office. Public expression took time and effort, and hopefully a lot of thought in the process.

I am realizing I've been conditioned to be the Pavlovian dog, to respond to stimuli in an expected, routine "in a New York minute" way, simply becoming a product of this age of advertising, manipulation, and conditioning.

But what if I was, instead, calm, supportive, caring, and expressed unconditional compassion and love? Perhaps just being present, in a kind way, should be my response to others in conflict and crisis. Can I just suspend judgement and criticism? Maybe not feeding my ego with my unappreciated and intrusive opinions when simply being there for someone and exuding gentle support and kindness would be much more appreciated and needed in the situation.

"You walk along with them without judgment, sharing their journey to an unknown destination. Yet you're completely willing to end up wherever they need to go. You give your heart, let go of control, and offer unconditional support."

---Lynn Hauka -- Coach

In life, we have numerous job titles and duties, and often, those are multiple roles, calling upon our experiences and our ability to navigate the complexities and subtleties of modern life. Being the son, the father, the uncle, the spouse, the friend, the mentor, the teacher, the confidante is a role more appropriate by just quietly being there for someone. Unwanted and often uninformed advice often taints the situation, and shame, guilt, and a sense of failure soon follows.

Holding space "…means that we are willing to walk alongside another person in whatever journey they're on without judging them, making them feel inadequate, trying to fix them, or trying to impact the outcome. When we hold space for other people, we open our hearts, offer unconditional support, and let go of judgement and control."

---Heather Plett

What the situation really often calls for is compassion and unconditional love, a holding of sacred space to just "let it be". That may not be what our culture seems to expect, yet it is a revolutionary and culture-changing response.

For me, I need to take a breath, and let it out slowly, taking my time to plan my response, and to put myself in the most effective position of the supporting, compassionate friend and listening post that the person in need is really needing to have around when the crisis is at hand.

We don't have to rush in, armed with our snap judgements and fire hose responses, issuing our breathless bulletins on social media, or even feeding the local gossip mill. Time is on our side and is an ally for the managers of crisis and personal angst. Time will tell if I need to voice an opinion, or give some wise counsel, and if I do, then the wait will be worthwhile, and the Universe will give me that guidance. And, I can frame the most appropriate, the most effective action.

Or, I can simply be there, offering support quietly, by my presence, exuding kindness and love and understanding, and offering the balm of friendship and compassion.

Silence, often, becomes the best tool, the most effective fix to the matter at hand. One kind, thoughtful, compassionate soul become an ally, rather than an unwelcome new factor, the volatile instigator of an even larger conflagration.

Simply by holding space, by being the calm in the storm, you can make a better world.

24 GRIEVING AND GROWING

The weeks before spring, before the world comes fully awake from its winter slumber and bursts forth with flowers and growth and new hope for a bright and joyous planet, is a time of contemplation for me. And now is a time for me to grieve, as lately I have lost some good friends.

Once again, the world is teaching me, and today's lessons are about loss and leaving, about life and what we are here for. Like everything else in the School of Life, I don't have much say in the curriculum or the class schedule. Yet, it is my job to show up and learn the lessons of the day.

My friends' time has come and they have moved on, leaving this world. I wasn't ready to say goodbye, but then, I never am. I can rage and scream and cry, but all that is not very productive. I still feel empty inside, and not really sure I know how to honor their lives. I look at how their lives have shaped my own, enriching me, and given me tools and ideas from which I can be a better person, and make a bigger difference in the world. There are always lessons to be learned, and ways for me to improve myself.

The spaces they filled in my life are empty, though I try to fill that up with something creative, something that will make a difference in this world, as if to make up for what they aren't doing in the world anymore. But, that's a fool's errand. I can't fill in the gaps that they have left in my life, and I can't duplicate what they did, or would be doing now if they hadn't died. Each of us is special, unique.

I don't think we are here to be clones of those who have moved on. Each of us has our own work to do here.

In my own life, though, I can better my own life, being more of a giver, a teacher, a creator, and a lover of the world. That's what my lately departed friends would want too, if they were sitting here having a cup of coffee with me. They'd be pretty insistent with me, not being people who would cry in their beer, or host a pity party on their untimely and undesired demise. They wouldn't want me to be doing that either.

"Get on with life," I can hear several of them say. "You've got more work to do. Now, get to it."

Look at what you have taught, what you have created with your hands, and how much love you have spread. That's the directive I'm getting from the Universe, as I wake to another day, and wonder, once again, what I am here for.

It's not my time yet to go. So I must go on. I must spend less time thinking about those tears in my beer, and get out into the world, get a move on. The departed ones are still with me, in many ways, and I still hear their voices, and their ideas and wisdom. They were in my life for many reasons, and it is up to me to discover all that they have given me in our all too brief time together on this planet.

I have much to learn. The days are getting longer now, and the sunshine is warmer. Spring is coming, and life is renewing. It is time for me to grow, and to love more than I have ever thought possible.

Another Day

Thoughts of you came again, out of the night's last blackness, the false dawn

Filling the eastern sky with the promises of a new day,

Time and fading night sky eroding our shared times together.

My gut clenches over you leaving so soon

When we'd just had gotten started, our coffee now grown cold

Cold as your grave.

Our conversations now are only one way,

My questions unanswered; you have fallen silent,

So unlike you, not to acknowledge what I have to say.

What are friends for?

Dawn's light grows brighter, waking the birds,

Lighting the new day with promise.

You ignore it all, not speaking up

Remaining silent and cold, so unlike the old you.

I can only cry.

25 --- ONE PERSON MAKING A DIFFERENCE

The daily news can be overwhelming, and often paralyzes me into a state of inaction, frustration, and disappointment on how I fit in. I wonder if my life really has meaning. Nothing I can do will make a difference, part of my brain rationalizes, pushing me into idleness and despondency.

I have to work hard to countermand that kind of thinking, which is ineffective and against all of my values and spirituality. I bring value to the world. Everyone does. Creating change and spreading love is the essence of my purpose on this planet. Yet, the negativity and depressive energy seems to be persistent and ever-present.

Others, with great wisdom, take on this feeling, this social attitude that often seems pervasive. They turn it around and urge us to be proactive, to initiate change by engaging with others. And, often that work is not a shout out to the entire world, but quiet, thoughtful work, one on one, giving an individual some attention and direction.

Oprah's new book, *The Path Made Clear: Discovering Your Life's Direction and Purpose,* is a delightful and inspiring collection of quotes and short essays on empowering yourself to change your attitude and the world.

"When you know, teach. When you get, give." – Maya Angelou.

We are all teachers and givers. That is what we are here for, the purpose of life. As a child, I found great joy in life in simply being with others. The greatest satisfactions came with experiences with others. Sharing, giving, teaching, it is all the same, moving us towards our purpose, our life force of one's love to others. I often get side-tracked and forget that profound lesson I learned as a child.

When we give, when we teach, when we share of ourselves to others, that spreads out into the world, like a pebble tossed into a pond. The good from that rebounds back to us, often in ways we may not recognize or even be aware. And, often that echoing is seen many years later, our initial altruistic act nearly forgotten.

The time frame for that fits no pre-conceived schedule or expectation. Often, I sense that "return on investment" as a surprise, a new, unexpected gift back to me.

At other times, my investment seems like a poor choice. The recipient of my attention, my nurturance and loving, acts out with meanness, anger, and multiple acts of self and social destruction and violence. I see numerous acts of narcissistic rage and self-harm, a desire to "win at all cost".

The addictions of this world, be it drugs, violence, selfishness, or other toxins, often can seem to be the winners on the battlefields people create to try to make it through our lives. I can't change the world by having bigger, more deadly weapons in my arsenal. Such escalation only increases the casualty lists and leaves the world poorer, more broken. Hatred is a no-win answer for any problem. And, it turns me into a nasty, vitriolic shell of my true self.

"There is no more neutrality in the world. You either have to be part of the solution, or you're going to be part of the problem." – Eldridge Cleaver.

If I am patient, and understanding, and willing to step to the side and let the storms of rage and loathing pass by, the inherent goodness can still be found in the ashes of the outcomes of frustration and acting out. In those moments, there is often a "sweet moment" of opportunity.

I try to turn it around, and rather than fling my own spears and shoot my own arrows of hostility and rage, I get in touch with my own gentle side, and respond with compassion, patience, and reaching out to them.

Such an approach is not without its challenges. But, I'm stubborn and persistent in my own path of being an instrument of change.

A few words of kindness, a smile, a warm and welcoming handshake can be disarming. If the recipient of my outreach responds with a look of need or even acknowledgement of my message, then the communication has begun, and the path of their day of anger and rage has been changed.

Just listening, with compassion, is a revolutionary act.

People do change. It is often a small change, but it IS a change, an alteration, a glimpse of an alternative on how one should feel, how the day can be navigated in a different way, even in developing a vision on living an intentional, purposeful life based upon love.

Perhaps in those small acts, I am a rebel, a revolutionary, going in a direction that isn't what is expected of me, or the place in this world other people perceive I should occupy.

"You reap what you sow."

I can be the good farmer, the good steward of my own heart and its bounty. If I take care of my own little corner of the world, and let my garden grow, then I can later share my harvest with the world.

When I reach out to someone and suspend judgement and bias, if I give of myself and my life force, then I'm being genuine, real, and open. That person I'm in touch with gets the real me, a person striving to be an honest, straight-forward bit of love and care, with all of my own imperfections and challenges.

Like all of us, I'm a work in progress.

That gift of me can help fill an empty spot, ease a pain, help heal a wound, even start a conversation.

"Someone cares" can also be a very powerful, world-changing message, a key ingredient in letting another person move closer to their true potential and find an easier path to their own peacefulness and gentleness.

We all need to heal. There are more than enough wounds in life that need to heal, to ease the pain in our hearts, to feel that we truly belong to our community, that our own life matters and has purpose.

I can make a difference. I am valued for what I do, who I am, and what I can contribute to others.

"Give to this world what you want to receive from the world, because that is what you will receive." --Gary Zukov

26 --- SEED PLANTING

Life, Beginning

Rough, wrinkled, like stone pebbles

Or round, smooth, perfect dark spheres

Or oblong, pointed, the arched ridges a seam

Or flaky, scales, the antithesis of juicy red ripe tomato.

So many choices, so many ways

To begin life, to thrust out roots and leaves

Stems and green aiming for the sun

And wiry roots pushing into the dirt, going down.

All they want from me is freedom,

Escaping the paper packets, to find the

Dirt

The light

And water

To just be with the longer days

And achieve their destiny.

I touch them, hold them,

Fingers sticky before they fall

Finding the dirt I've set out for them,

Starting them on their journey.

Being a builder of community is being a gardener, finding the "right spot", preparing the soil, selecting the seeds, being a nurturer. This work of gardening requires patience and determination.

The gardener doesn't always see the harvest of one's labors, but the world does.

27 --- THE GIFT OF SOBRIETY

"I know my limit," one young man kept saying, his bloodshot eyes and pale complexion seemingly at odds with his statement, as he held his energy drink, hands trembling. We were both in line at a store, he and his friends rehashing last night's alcohol-soaked party. They boasted to each other about last night's consumption, getting through hangovers, and the drunk friend who "overdid it".

Addiction doesn't care.

"It reverberates through the whole family, affecting entire generations for years," a friend recently told me. "Our kids saw that, and it affected each of them. Some were drawn to drinking like a moth to the flame; others were repulsed and became angry and bitter about their childhood. The devastation was so widespread, and we are still dealing with it."

Give the gift of sobriety this season.

This gift is not a gift to someone else. It is a gift to you, from you. Others won't respond to your preaching and your nagging, except to become even more entrenched in their behavior.

Give sobriety to yourself. Put some distance between you and the behavior, the "stinking thinking". Enjoy the quiet when that clutter has been moved to a safe distance away from your corner of the world.

Take care of yourself. Nurture yourself. Spend some quality time with the real you. Surround yourself with the things you truly enjoy. Indulge in the simple pleasures that you hold dear and treasure. Know your limits for addictive thinking and action.

Find acceptance in the silence, away from the chaos and noise. Find the genuine you; that person is an old friend. Honor the innate, fundamental goodness that is your very essence. Love yourself, for you are worthy of that love.

Being sober isn't just about one's consumption of alcohol and other drugs. It is about clear thinking, about avoiding the pitfalls of untruths, propaganda, and self-aggrandizement. When we adopt falsehoods and fashion our lives around deceptions and lies, we lose our direction in life, our ability to fashion a life based on reality and honesty. Being honest with ourselves is perhaps our most challenging task, but, in the end, coming to grips with what is really true truly serves ourselves and our souls.

At its heart, sobriety is clear thinking and the pursuit of being honest with yourself. Recognize the agendas and intentions of others to trick you, manipulate you and tempt you to serve the ulterior and selfish motives of others. Addiction enjoys the company, but it really doesn't care about you.

Be true to yourself. Search for the truth, as brutal and loud as it may be. Ignoring truth chips away at our souls and keeps us from finding and loving our true selves. Seeing one's own truth is the path to freedom.

Attitude

"Bending to a common purpose is more important than arising from a common place." David Treuer, *The Heartbeat of Wounded Knee: Native America from 1890 to the Present.*

I was recharged the other day at a planning session for a non-profit organization I participate in. We volunteers are mostly "retired", but collectively we are very active, and deeply involved in several meaningful activities throughout the community. We come from a variety of occupations and experiences, and have each decided to improve our knowledge, be better in the practice of the activities of the organization, and to educate the community.

To begin to be a part of the organization, one is required to take an intensive series of classes for nearly three months, complete with lectures, discussions, homework and practical skill applications. We are taught by experts and read professionally prepared study materials. At the end of this work, we need to pass a comprehensive written exam that tests our knowledge and our ability to research answers.

Our service work entails helping the public with their questions and problems in our area of interest. Great discussions ensue in this work, further sharpening our minds and improving our diagnostic and analytical skills.

Our work and fun is not all about the science and the advancement of our area of interest. We socialize and plan a variety of events that are both fun and educational, engaging the public, but also engaging us in fellowship and camaraderie. We savor the joy in our work and service.

Once a year, we dig into the mission and policies of our organization, taking a bird's eye view of what we do, why we do it, and wonder how we can do it better. We are generally detail oriented, so this day requires us to pull away from the details and look at how we can work better together and really serve the public interest.

It is often said in our community that life is all about relationships. This organization develops strong and productive interactions, and the building of friendships and collaborations. The work we do and the leadership training and experience spreads out to other organizations in the community. "Graduates" of our program are in leadership positions in many other organizations, and our problem-solving skills are an asset to the community.

One of the unwritten missions of this organization is having a positive attitude. Negativity and feeling defeated is not part of the organizational culture. We are solution-oriented, and we don't spend much time feeling sorry for ourselves or commiserating on something that has been unsatisfactory. Disappointment and "failure" is seen as a challenge to figure out why something didn't work, and then to move forward and strategize on what will likely work in the future.

We keep refining the "wheel" of our work, making it better, and changing with the times.

This attitude is self-reinforcing. We build on our networking and our successful models and grow our capacity to do our work in the community more productively.

One of the fuels we use is that our work is based upon scientific research. Our problem-solving work with community members who come to us with their challenges in our field of expertise is based upon scientific research. Our advice and our problem-solving is evidence-based research, and an examination of all of the causal factors, and our knowledge of local conditions and situations.

Problems are examined and solved collectively, with rich discussions and conversations, sometimes over a period of time.

"I'm not sure," is an acceptable short-term answer, but we keep looking, examining, and analyzing. We test our hypotheses and reach out to others in the know, looking for additional expertise and approaches. Being mistaken or "wrong" is not criticized but viewed as an integral part of our process. We encourage lively debates and discussions and realize that the science and the methodology is ever-changing and, hopefully, improving.

Our presence in the community has been a model of different ways to think about other community issues and problems. Our adoption of evidence-based research and scientific methods of analysis and thinking about issues has stirred others up to looking at our process as a better model of how organizations function, and the role they play in the community.

This power of education, and self-examination of how we think about something, is bringing positive results. Other groups have sprung up, using science and collaborative evaluation and thinking about a problem have yielded similar effective solutions. More people have been educated about scientific analysis and problem-solving, and this approach is now not only socially significant, but is becoming one of the models of how we go about living together and working through challenging problems.

This kind of work, this model of problem-solving requires us to change our thinking and to change our attitudes.

28 --- CHANGING MY ATTITUDE

A friend recently asked me how can we change, how can we transform ourselves from who we are, into something that is less of what we don't like about ourselves. What will be our legacy? How will we be remembered? How can we become our best?

"When you die, only three things will remain of you, since you will abandon all material things on the threshold of the Otherworld: what you have taught to others, what you have created with your hands, and how much love you have spread. So learn more and more in order to teach wise, long-lasting values. Work more and more to leave to the world things of great beauty. And love, love, love people around you for the light of love heals everything."

--- Francois Bourillon

Our creativity is a force, not only to fuel the light in our hearts, but to give light to others, to express thoughts that perhaps are inadequately expressed by words. Rather, we communicate with the light in our souls. Our own creativity, our own ways of expressing love, are unique to ourselves, and we are in control of that process, that message that we choose to share.

"But should you continue to be a respectful and helpful neighbor to her? Yes you should. Your behavior should reflect who you are, not who she is."

--Advice columnist Ask Amy

"We have to change our thinking.

"…how to move forward into the future in such a way as to not leave the past behind, to once and forever destroy the idea that to live one kind of life meant shedding the other; and to find some productive balance between growth and violence, between destruction and regeneration."

--Bobby Matthews, quoted in *The Heartbeat of Wounded Knee: Native America from 1890 to the Present,* (2019) by David Treuer

Each of our journeys is unique, wholly owned by ourselves, and what we learn from this, and how we choose to express our knowledge and our wisdom is ours alone to communicate and share.

Today, I am a different person from who I was yesterday. And, tomorrow, I will again be different, changed, transformed by today, and tomorrow, and also all that is in my past, my origins, the society in which I have lived my life.

The past is part of me, yet I can choose how I let it be a part of me, how it may be the cause of who I am, and who I am becoming. The past is a teacher, and, at times, a guide, but it is not my god, it is not directing me, nor does it command me to follow a certain path. There are many paths to wisdom and knowledge, and I am able to choose the paths that will best shape and enlighten my own journey.

Our community's economy is natural resource based. Historically, we have relied upon fishing, timber, and farming to be the foundation of our economy and our way of life. Environmental challenges, as well as being part of a global economy, have compelled us to deal with change on every level of our culture and our economy.

How our ancestors fished, logged and farmed is no longer viable, and we do things differently now. There are different expectations, different models, and different approaches.

These changes are unsettling and require new ways of thinking.

Over the past twenty years, changes in climate and development have resulted in increasing problems with winter flooding. Floods have become more severe and disruptive to our transportation and our economy. The affected interests were competitive and, at times, created impasses in conversations and thinking about solutions. Everyone was literally at the table for these problems, but we came about at it with old ways of thinking, and often anger and an unwillingness to listen to each other. Numerous "camps" of interest dug in their heels and solutions seemed unlikely and were viewed with hostility and animosity.

Wise leaders moved the conversation forward, seeking mediation and interest-based thinking and bargaining. Collaboration was advanced as a method that we could all benefit from.

The process was sweetened with federal and state dollars that were conditioned upon working together, being collaborative, and looking at a collective, community-wide solution. With the money on the table, and a growing pressure to not only find a solution but solutions tied to being able to work together, a "grand bargain" began to take shape.

Questions and dilemmas were re-defined as collective challenges and opportunities to improve our lives. The negatives became positives. The view of the issues being "win-win", rather than "us vs them" brought about a change in thinking.

Personal attitudes and posturing shifted, as the leadership in community thinking modeled new approaches and new modalities of problem solving. Successes in other communities were studied, and some of the participants in those resolved conflicts interacted with key players, on an individual basis.

The leadership also worked to develop personal rapport with the more vocal and strident players, making sure there were times for some one-on-one conversations, and opportunities to "walk a mile in the shoes" of their adversaries. Workplaces were visited, meetings were held over coffee, and people were exposed to each other's lives on a personal and intimate basis. There was an atmosphere shift in that we had more in common with each other than we had differences.

Stories were told of lives affected by the flooding, with environmental activists and scientists engaging in rescuing cows from flood waters and helping to clean up homes that had been flooded out. Local media featured stories on those affected by flooding. And people heard stories of how proposed changes actually worked in other communities.

The fear of change was eased because of these conversations and experiences.

It was not always an easy and joyful process. There was a lot of give and take, and compromises and mutual understandings did not always come about easily. The leadership kept the paths of community communication open. Difficult relationships slowly changed into more collaborative styles. The fatigue of conflict and lack of resolution also worked its magic, becoming a driving force of "let's get this done".

Parts of the "grand bargain" began to be funded and implemented, and some of the fears that the solutions would be a disaster began to fade.

Another flood occurred, somewhat minor in scope, but it was an opportunity to see how the solution could work. And, it did. There were some actual benefits that resulted from working together and trying something new. The engineering work was validated, and the small kernels of trust and cooperation began to grow.

There was also a shift in the dynamics of the community, as newcomers came here seeing the cooperation, the research, and saw it as the norm of community dynamics. There was an expectation that people worked together, that the problems had solutions. So, let's move forward. The old thinking was just history and not what we need to have in our community here today.

Working together and being collaborative was finally seen as a useful approach and has become a cultural norm.

The question of whether we should have flood control and reconfigure our estuaries to a better model and plan is no longer a question for the community. That question has been answered, and we are moving ahead.

Not that we don't still disagree on environmental issues. We still have serious and often divisive debates. But those conversations have shifted away from flood management and estuary health to deeper, more regional and national conflicts on the environment, climate change, food production, timber management, and political philosophies. The healthy relationships fostered during the conversations about flood management continue, with the realization that we can talk with each other about tough issues, and solutions can be found that will accommodate the concerns and needs of most everyone involved.

I choose to build community, to find strength, determination, purpose, and resiliency. In seeking others to be my compatriots and fellow journeyers, the question of where we each have come from seems to matter less and less to me. More important is the direction that we are going.

29 --- SMALL TOWN LIFE

Hot coffee in a café where the waitress knows your name and how you like your coffee.

Visiting with friends and neighbors at the post office, where the clerk knows your box number and where you live.

Taking an extra half hour at the grocery store, as you run into friends, and do a little business, connecting.

Talking about where something is at, and referring to homeowners, farmers, and businesses that haven't been there for at least twenty years.

Patiently giving a tourist directions to the major sites and realizing they really don't know where the beach is. And resenting all the visitors and the traffic, yet also realizing that people come here for the amazing beauty which you take for granted every day.

Being grumpy about a slow-moving line of traffic when you are headed home, then seeing the herd of elk that everyone has stopped for.

Sitting next to a high school classmate, talking about our retired life, and realizing our grandmothers were friends.

Realizing that you remember all the businesses that have been at a location throughout your life, and that you are now the geezer that you laughed at when you were a kid. "How does he know all of that about this town?" you asked your folks, and now you know. Geezerhood is an acquired skill.

Driving by the "new" high school you went to, realizing that it was built seventy years ago, and that your friends' grandchildren are students.

Giving your neighbor a few jars of your gooseberry jam as he keeps bringing you a dozen eggs from his chickens every couple of weeks. You give a sharp look to the strange car that goes up their driveway and make a mental note of the license plate and who was driving.

Looking through the weekly paper, realizing that you already know the news, but you're reading the letters to the editor and the obituaries, because that's what people at the coffee shop are going to be talking about.

Waving to the UPS driver and the mail carrier, as they waved at you first and know where you live.

30 --- A DAY OF KINDNESS

I had a big dose of soul medicine and human kindness last winter. The experience restored my faith in humanity and the power of unconditional love. I saw my community at its best.

A friend invited me to *Homeless Connect*, a community effort to provide basic needs to those among us who find themselves without shelter and other necessities.

The weather was bitter. Cold winds blew and temperatures were in the 20s at night. It wasn't so rough that the local warming shelter would be open, but it was still promising to be a miserable night.

My task was to be the greeter and the poll taker as folks left.

"Did you get what you needed?" and "What could we do better?"

I met a steady stream of people, people of all ages and circumstances. I didn't know their stories, and that kind of personal information was thankfully unwanted. We simply welcomed everyone who showed up and took care of basic needs. The red tape of bureaucracy was nowhere to be found. We did keep track of how many people came, as those without shelter are nearly invisible in our culture.

I saw a lot of smiles. Their pets were cared for, vaccinated, and fed. They had a hot meal and haircuts, were tended by health care providers, and connected with services by nearly every social service agency in town. They could pick up clean, warm clothes, blankets, sleeping bags, shoes, coats, tarps, and tents.

They made connections, not just with people and agencies who could offer a helping hand, but also with each other.

I saw connections made and strengthened with friends, family, an abundance of job prospects and housing tips. There was a spirit of fellowship and camaraderie filling the church gym where we had all gathered.

People were helping people, giving a helping hand, a ride, ideas and where to get help for a particular problem, connecting with others who cared. There was dignity and love.

It was an afternoon of suspended judgement and the absence of loudly voiced opinions and political rhetoric, blaming and stereotyping. Instead, it was a time of getting the right size of winter coat, a sleeping bag, a bag of food for someone's dog, a haircut, a hot meal, and a tip on a decent, safe place to pitch a tent.

Everyone helped everyone else. No one left without something to help them take better care of themselves, make their lives a little easier, and a feeling that they were an important part of the community.

Community. That was the unpublished message of the day. People had generously donated the food, clothing, bedding, pet care, medical care, and an afternoon of services to reach out to and help their fellow community members.

There were great conversations, interactions on problem solving and connecting people to each other, sharing resources and knowledge, being human and acting with kindness and compassion. There was respect.

The sun moved lower and the cold wind off the mountains pushed deeper through my coat, reminding me that night was coming. The people I was talking with were slowly drifting away, off to spend this night sleeping on the ground, with maybe only a tarp, a tent, and a sleeping bag to ward off the frosty air, and the loneliness of yet another night without permanent shelter.

I struggled to relate, to comprehend their lives. I knew that I had a warm home to return to when my volunteer shift came to an end. There would be family to greet me, a hot meal on the stove, a comfortable chair, a good book, a warm, clean bed, and a bathroom with hot water and clean towels. I would not have to move on when the sun came up, putting all of my possessions into a plastic garbage bag, and maybe a backpack, and wondering where my next meal was coming from.

Also at home would be my assumptions about life, about meeting a person's basic needs and how people live in our community.

I assume a lot, yet I'm complacent, ignorant about how so many people in our community live, what they don't have, and what they can expect in the days to come. I find myself too often acting blind to the dilemma of such need in a society where some are wealthy, and there is an abundance of necessities, yet out of reach of so many.

For that afternoon at least, there was compassion, service, charity, and a common fellowship of people helping each other, of making lives more comfortable, more bearable. Another cold winter's night was coming, and dedicated community members had made a small effort to help ease people's circumstances, maybe helping them step forward into better times.

I learned, again, that in our humanity, it is not difficult to act with kindness and compassion. If I suspend judgement and comparison, if I try to walk a mile in another's shoes, then I can look at the world with greater understanding.

And, I can renew myself, and again be connected to the true purpose of our lives.

31 --- THE COMMUNITY BEHIND BARS

The United States imprisons 2.2 million people, with 6.6 million people "in the system" (prison, parole, probation). The system is racially biased, with 67% of the prison population being people of color, compared to 37% in society generally.

The costs are staggering. Oregon spends over $1 Billion on prisons, with 15,200 behind bars, and an additional 60,000 people on parole or probation.

What does this community look like, and how does one build it? My friend, Derek Ellwood, is a long-term inmate in an Oregon prison. He is a poet, and a passionate writer. We exchange letters, poems, and essays, and I have seen him grow as a writer and as a compassionate, focused young man.

"As we consider the strengths behind community building, most people might view this objective as a way to improve our surroundings as a whole. That in itself would be true, but community building also has the benefit of greatly improving an individual's character. Their ability to participate in something gives them a sense of belonging; where in fact they may have felt alienated before.

"Being incarcerated, I have had to navigate the treacherous waters of community building, under strenuous circumstances, on several occasions. The communities in prison tend to have a bit of distinct obstacles that make transitions into certain communities more difficult, as opposed to ones outside of prison. But I can clearly see how the benefits of building community inside contrasted with outside can closely relate to one another.

"Community building, when employed properly, can be a powerful and effective tool in making the worst situations better and serve as a model of success for others to follow.

"Some of the barriers to building a healthy community inside prison include race, sexual identity, gang status, criminal category, as well as just being different. Affluential status can also be a hinderance to building community. Yet the most significant obstruction to this objective is inclusivity or rather, the lack of being inclusive. This form of tribalism does nothing more than banish us to our corners of ideology.

"Aside from gang influence and criminal categorizing, the impediment that causes us to not create healthy, thriving communities are not that different from free society's challenges.

"We should not shirk our responsibility to build community because there are challenges. In fact, this may be the very reason we should be building community.

"I would regard building community similar to making a cake; where each individual brings a unique skill set, character trait, and special ingredient to the community. However, if left as an entity to themselves, may not be all that palatable. Nevertheless, when combined with all the other ingredients and in the correct amounts, the results can prove to be pretty spectacular.

"When an individual is involved in the building of a community, then tend to be more engaged and discover what their talents are as well as their strengths. They also have the advantage of obtaining positive character traits of others in the group.

"Another benefit to participating in community building is people are inclined to gain a sense of pride from creating something and being a part of that creation. By developing a sense of pride, an individual will embrace their responsibility to the project. When they have a sense of pride, they won't want to let their other project members down.

"Although there are several benefits and layers to building community, I think the most important issue is inclusivity. When someone is not included in a community setting, the very fabric of the community is destined to fail. A person who is not included feels ostracized and lost. In that instance, this member may act in a manner that jeopardizes the success of the community. When one member fails, the community fails.

"If we can learn to set aside our prejudices and include all people in our efforts to build a successful and sustainable community, we will have supplied the one ingredient that "binds the cake" (us) together ---- compassion."

---Derek Ellwood

What is often forgotten in conversations about criminals, the "system", and societal woes, is that almost all prisoners eventually get out and need to find a place in society. I've been involved in mentoring young men in prison and being the guy that picks them up at the prison gate to take them on the next step of their journey. All too often, the resources for them are meager to non-existent.

Here's my story about one such trip I took with a young man.

Traveling With Joseph

Not everyone is prison has support from their family. I have volunteered at the Oregon Youth Authority prison in my town, and I spend time with young men who don't have their families in their lives.

When they get paroled, and it is time for them to leave, there is no one to pick them up. Picking them up from the prison gate and taking them to their new lives is one of my jobs. I call it Freedom Day.

Freedom Day starts at 6 a.m., and the gate slams behind us, the last time for Joseph. He is free.

"Wow, first time without shackles," he says, his voice trembling with emotion.

We don't know where Joseph will sleep tonight. The parole bureaucracy hasn't figured that out, though they've known for the last seven years that he's getting out today. Another uncertainty for this big day. He'll end up tonight at a retched, flea bag motel on the edge of town, surrounded by meth addicts and drunks, without a key to his room. And, I'll be angry about it, but that's the way it goes. Another indignity. More disrespect.

Joseph is bright. He's earned his associate's degree and is the prison camp's technology wizard. He's planning to get his bachelor's degree in computer programming and is already enrolled at the university in his hometown.

We've got 200 miles to go, but I take him to the beach first, so he can take a walk without handcuffs and belly chains and breathe the fresh salt air for the first time in seven years. I stay in the pickup and let him walk down to the beach by himself. It's his first time to be alone in all that time.

We stop for coffee and I talk him into a cinnamon roll. He tries to not ask for anything from me, but I'm dad today, and he needs some fatherly care. He laughs at the metal fork, his first time not eating with plastic in seven years. Everything today is so new.

Driving into the mountains, we follow a river, his eyes soaking up the sunlight on the water, the rapids, and the misty, clean air of a perfect June day. He stares at it all, sometimes asking a question about the fish, the trees, and deeper questions, about college, and life, and who he wants to become.

By the road, there's been a big forest fire last year, lots of blackened trees, new baby trees, and wildflowers. It's a rich metaphor: devastation, replanting, renewal, all the possibilities of a new life. He falls silent, taking it all in, learning the lessons of nature.

We stop at the summit to look at a few of the peaks of the mountains. We smell wild roses, pine trees, and crisp mountain air, scented with last night's rainfall. A hawk flies in the distance, and a tear rolls down his face.

I cry, too, holding him tight, as he tells me how he's missed these mountains, these smells, the hawk soaring high into the blue sky the last seven years, a third of his life. He breaks down and sobs, his chest gasping the cool thin air, his tears soaking my shirt.

We fall silent, and I feel his heartbeat, his arms clutching me tight. On Freedom Day, there are often no words.

Two hours in the parole office, filling out endless forms, getting a lecture on all the rules, finding out that his home is the fleabag motel. He's pretty calm about it all, telling me he can deal with it. He's going to succeed, despite all of the rules and all of the barriers thrown in his way.

We get him settled in. He'll be OK, he tells me.

"Don't worry. I'll be fine," he says.

Before prison, he lived in the woods one winter, and I know he's determined.

There's one last task before I leave. He needs a bike. He'd built a bike from scrap metal at prison, but we didn't have room for it in the car, and it didn't have any pedals.

I told him I'd buy him a bike, once we got to his hometown. He needed it for college, and for work.

"No, don't get me anything. Don't be nice to me. I don't deserve it," he said.

I hand him an envelope; the money for his bike.

Joseph gulps and looks down, giving me that bad puppy after it peed on the carpet and chewed up my shoe look.

"I want to do this," I said. "I'm not letting you say no, son. You can pay me back some day, or pay it forward, if you think you owe me."

He takes the envelope, counting out the money a couple of times, before folding it in his wallet. He gets quiet, and I look away when I see a tear slide down his face.

I get quiet, too. I do that when I get angry. And, I'm angry about a father and a family who aren't in their son's life, who don't show up on Freedom Day, about not visiting him for seven years. I get angry about them not keeping him in school, about letting him live in the woods when he's sixteen. And, I'm angry about the flea bag motel he's going back to tonight, and not having a lock for his door, and for all the time he's been in prison.

I cried when I left him that sunny June day, a day so vibrant and fresh, when you think anything is possible. He grinned and gave me a big wave, as I watched him ride his shiny red bike down the road, into the rest of his beautiful, young life.

There's a follow up story, too, four years later. Joseph found two jobs, fell in love, and married. He bought a car. They had a son, and he earned his bachelor's degree. He has a busy life, with work and fatherhood. There's always a big smile on his face when he shares some family photos with me.

Last year, he let me know that he didn't need his bike anymore, and gave it to a co-worker, who needed a way to get back and forth to work. He paid it forward, and he makes me proud of who he has become.

32 --- A GROVE OF FORESTERS

Community is found everywhere. One Sunday afternoon, I found myself in a grove of foresters, gathered for an annual lecture series.

The goal of the organizers was to hear from younger foresters and showcase new ideas and new ways of thinking about the issues in the field of forestry. Professionals from governments, timber companies, non-profits, and other people interested in natural resource management came together for conversation, stimulating discussions, and looking at trends with fresh and enthusiastic eyes.

Strident, hot-blooded political talk was discouraged and instead we focused on observations, established facts and thinking outside of the box in this vital natural science and essential national industry.

The Hagenstein Lectures are an annual event held at the World Forestry Center in Portland, Oregon and sponsored by the World Forestry Center and the American Society of Foresters.

W. D. "Bill" Hagenstein was a larger-than-life character, world forester, scientist, author, visionary, and a tireless champion of long-view forest management to provide tangible environmental, social, and economic benefits. Recognized as the father of native tree reforestation in the Pacific Northwest, Hagenstein was an active, working forester for more than 75 years. He was national president of the Society of American Foresters and a founder of the World Forestry Center in 1966. Hagenstein was highly respected, brutally honest, a magnetic storyteller, and a shameless advocate. He was awarded the prestigious Gifford Pinchot Medal in 1986. Hagenstein died in Portland, Oregon at age 99 in 2014."
https://hagensteinlectures.org.

He believed in good conversations and intelligent discussions and analysis, where ideas could be freely shared respectfully. Good food and drink were also essential, and those niceties are an essential part of the afternoon.

While the presentations were invigorating, and the speakers carefully chosen for their perspectives, experience, and ability to engage others, the conference center became a noisy place during the breaks, where networking and discussion about the lectures were lively and exciting.

It was invigorating to me to see people from all perspectives and experience mingle, excited about new trends, and fresh scientific studies of natural resource issues.

I listened intently, with some of the terms and perspectives unfamiliar to me. While I'm an avid reader of natural resource issues in the mainstream media, much of the discussions were cutting edge to me, with perspectives based on "boots on the ground" experiences and unpublished research.

Many in the audience knew each other, and eagerly engaged with each other and the speakers. It was time for me to sit back and take it all in, marveling at the depth of knowledge and experience in the room.

Wildfire Management

Collective wisdom can be subjective and ultimately flawed.

In the 1920s, the collective wisdom in forest management was to actively suppress forest fires, which allowed the volume of flammable materials to accumulate, increasing the risk of larger and hotter fires, and conflagrations. The native American practice of small controlled burns was rejected as being "primitive", even though that approach resulted in small fires and forests that were more open and more productive in terms of timber yields.

In the 1990s, that management model changed, in favor of small controlled "prescriptive" burns that reduced fuel loads. This change in thinking is leading to healthier forests, and forest fire management that has reduced the risk of conflagrations. Of course, there are other significant factors, including climate change, increasing temperatures, declines in rainfall, logging patterns, and increasing residential use of forested properties.

The "wildfire paradox" is a complex mix of historical management, climate change, public demand for higher and more aggressive fire suppression. Fire is both a problem and a solution. We need to learn to live with wildland fire, as it will always be a factor.

Forestry science is challenged to restructure the forest, and foster resilience and adaptation to fire. The wildfire environment is increasingly complex, and we are challenged to align land management actions with wildlife response.

Today, foresters are reintroducing fire to improve forest health. Science is combined with art and dealing with the unexpected. Foresters strive for finding the right treatment, the right place, and the right time.

Wildfire is inevitable. Now, there are compounding dynamics, and all groups need to be involved in the conversation. Recognize that our current efforts on fire suppression are only 100 years old. Active forest management requires a whole range of treatment, being open minded, and adaptive to a variety of approaches.

Challenges for Mid-level Managers in the Middle of Their Careers

What is the relevancy today for the academic learning of twenty years ago? Managers are challenged to create a community that welcomes diversity of approaches and build an environment where people can thrive, and not be isolated. Foresters' work and their "laboratory" is in forests, which are, by their nature, rural, isolated, and untamed.

Trust building is essential, within the profession, and with others. Building trust in a rural community is challenging and requires bridge building across a variety of diverse interests.

What motivates mid-career foresters today?

There is a need to collaborate among stakeholders, community members, and academia.

What has led us to the most urgent problems we have? Forests interplay with science, policy, nature, and practicality, and this interplay is more of an art than a precise science. This interplay is the motivating force; not the need to be confrontational. The core question is "what makes sense".

Foresters should foster a sense of curiosity and a sense of community, working for the common good. We get lost in the technical details, and we need to convey a sense of value and commonality. We need a commonality of passion and community across professions and knowledge bases. Good forestry requires a global vision, literally "seeing the forest for the trees".

One of our strengths is to not respond in the moment, not be combative. We do not need to feel personally attacked, and to recognize there is the idea, and there is the personality.

We need to bring ourselves to the situation, and recognize the guard rails, the boundaries, and be aware. Are the guard rails changing? Yes. Our motivation is there, and what hurts the most is when you hit the ground the hardest, when you are the most passionate.

Our search is for common ground, open to the diversity of opinions, and be comfortable in saying "it depends". We often don't know the answer, but we should know the question.

There is comfort in learning something new, and also to be uncomfortable with what you thought you knew, and it turns out to be something else. We need to be willing to go out on a limb and take a risk.

Sometimes, we need to ask the simple questions.

Our challenges:

- There is a lag between what we see changing and what has already changed.
- Communication. We come from different perspectives, different views, opinions, and knowledge bases.
- We don't always create an effective narrative.
- There are challenges and there are opportunities.
- Show the world our toolbox is full, robust, and ever expanding. In doing that, we ear trust, and show that we are open to new tools, and we are broadening our toolbox.
-

I know that other professions have similar gatherings, formal or informal, challenging each other on significant issues in their field, and engage in vigorous discussions. Resolution and agreement aren't required, but honest, intellectual discussion and analysis is, and the profession advances because people take the time to come together and take on the tough subjects.

I've attended some of those meetings, as well as meetings in my old professional field. I come away invigorated and gratified that there are so many thoughtful people in the world, people who readily admit they don't have all of the answers, but they have lots of questions.

Just when I think I might know most of what there is to know in this world on a particular subject, I have a conversation with someone on the cutting edge of the issue, someone who is up to their eyeballs in the challenges of the day.

No, I don't know everything, I find out. In fact, I know very little sometimes. What I thought I knew, and what has been perceived as solid, "take it to the bank" knowledge about how the problem is managed and what we know about how things work, turns out not to be so. Truth and believability are in motion, ever-changing. Assumptions need to be re-examined, re-analyzed, as the world changes, thinking changes, and people often ask the questions that should make us rethink and re-examine some of the most basic understandings and beliefs.

Days later after the forestry lectures, I was thinking about forest management and fire.

I live on the edge of forest land that was the scene of a series of enormous devastating fires in the 1930s to the 1950s. Hundreds of thousands of prime timber land burned and reburned, and we thought it was a cataclysmic disaster. A beautiful forest was now covered in ash and burned trees, and very little greenery seemed to exist. Yet, over my lifetime, these forests have regenerated, and today, it is difficult to imagine that most of the county I call home was a burnt and desolate landscape.

Forests recover and regenerate. It is the cycle of life. We've learned that periodic fires are part of the natural cycle, that fire has its place in the health of the forest. Forests are ever-changing, and rely upon fire as one process, one event, that has its place in the development and changes that forests naturally go through.

We are alarmed at the horrific fires in California, yet fire is a very large part of the natural cycle of that area of the world. Yes, we are experiencing climate change, and there are now more fires than there have been in the recent past.

Yet, repressing fires and not allowing periodic burns may have contributed to the calamity of the recent fires, because of a buildup in fuels. We've also built homes and other structures in the forests, and installed regional electrical power grids, adding to the potential for starting fires and rural homes being subjected to the ravages of fire.

The public relations image of Smokey the Bear, which taught me as a child that forest fires are bad and need to be repressed, is now outdated, and seen as a simplistic concept in the field of forestry.

One government forester at the lectures explained her job as "starting more fires than I put out."

We get set in our ways and continue to stick to old ideas and concrete thinking. If we shun new information and new approaches, and don't engage in thoughtful dialogue and discussion with our colleagues, our old ways will be left behind and we will be intellectually and morally dishonest.

You don't need a college degree to be able to look at the world or a particular problem in a new way. Everyone can be observant, thoughtful, and be a challenger of the status quo, the established ways of thinking about a topic.

It is easy to forget that we have a choice every day. We can look at the facts, and our experiences, and look outside of the box sometimes, embracing new thoughts, and start an engaging and energetic discussion.

We can wonder "what if".

33 --- THE WORK TO BE DONE

My community recently celebrated. We celebrated a vibrant business community, a community replete with institutions and activities that engage and strengthen our community. We honored progressive, hard-working leaders, and successful businesses.

We celebrated our creative arts and talents, gathering in several venues to share our music, our poetry, our sense of community. We sang, and many of us listened to the words of Martin Luther King, Jr., and rededicating ourselves to social justice and personal commitment to change and betterment.

People gathered in classrooms, churches, and community halls, working to improve their skills and knowledge, learning how to better their lives and their communities.

Students shared their accomplishments, in tournaments and games, and in their community service work.

Yet, there is work to be done.

At these same celebrations, where the talents and intellect of individuals were honored, people overindulged in alcohol, were high on street drugs, and became boorish and obnoxious. They put their lives and the lives of others at risk by driving, and making other foolish, impulsive decisions, some of them life-altering.

They anxiously awaited the arrival of their drug deals at the local rest area, strung out and jittery, a lonely, rainy evening spent looking for their next high, rather than being home parenting their child.

They camped in tents in the woods and under bridges, unable to find or afford adequate housing, being hungry and cold, deserted by the world.

They looked into bare cupboards and refrigerators, unable to afford adequate food for their families, their hard-earned wages simply not enough to meet their basic needs.

They were sick, yet do not have adequate access to health care, and the medicines they and their children need, often overwhelmed and shut out by a bureaucracy, and a mindset of profit rather than serving the needs of the sick.

They lived in fear, their homes afflicted with violence and rage, often fueled by alcoholism, drugs, mental illness, and overwhelming anger and hopelessness.

Some gathered together, to spread fear and uncertainly, bias and prejudice, dividing people into neat categories of "us" and "them", and rationalizing the differences. They have rationalized why the "others" should be segregated and kept apart, why hate and disrespect should guide our political choices, and the way we treat others. Some have forgotten the tools for searching for the truth, for living their lives with love and compassion.

There is complacency, making it easy to change the "we" and "us", to "they" and "them", to look the other way, and to think that it is only me who knows the real truth.

"The ultimate tragedy is not the oppression and cruelty by the bad people, but the silence over that by the good people." – Martin Luther King, Jr.

"If you are good, yet silent, maybe you're not really as good as you think." – Leonard Pitts.

We live in an age of an overwhelming abundance of information, easily accessed by devices we carry in our pockets, or from the comfort of our couches. Knowledge and connection are literally at our fingertips; yet we so often do not know how to communicate, and how to love and care for ourselves, our families, and our neighbors. In all this abundance, we are often lonely and without purpose to our lives.

It's not not knowing the problem, the issues, the causes, or even the remedies.

The solutions lie in our personal and collective will to be the change makers, to reach into our own souls and to reach out to others, to strengthen our collective abilities to heal, to rectify, and to build a society that aligns with the values we profess to hold so dear.

Our work is not done.

That work takes intention, determination, and commitment, from every one of us.

Befriending

Kindness

Comes in so many forms, so many ways

A smile, a cup of tea,

Reaching out, giving a hand

Listening

Accepting.

Together

We honor ourselves and each other

Gifts to share, building community

Bonds, interactions, communion

Union, reciprocity

Strengthening, a weaving together

The whole greater than the parts.

Compassion

Understanding the Other, each other

By opening our own hearts

Being open, exchanging, offering

Receiving

Accepting

Enhancing

Uniting.

34 --- BEING INVITING: THE EXTRA CHAIR

An aspect of a healthy community is including a wide range of people in decision making and community affairs.

"Many hands make light work" is a popular proverb, yet there's the converse of that, from Margaret Mead: "Never doubt that a small group of thoughtful, committed citizens can change the world; indeed, it's the only thing that ever has."

These two ideas appear to be in conflict, yet they convey two sides of the coin of community building and involvement. Change happens when a small group of people can envision a better world, a better way of looking at a problem. They break down the problem into small pieces, and then strategize possible solutions. Collectively, they can test those solutions and identify the steps needed to implement their chosen path.

Then, they move ahead, putting their solutions in play and start working the problem. Their power comes from working together, engaging in collective thinking and also thinking outside of the box, outside of the "old ways" that may not have thoroughly addressed the problem.

Small groups can mobilize others, and people advance their new thinking. Progress can be observed and measured. Collaboration ensues.

The world today demands new innovative approaches to age old problems. We have astonishing access to information and communication, yet we often ignore the power of a small group of creative thinkers and doers. We also undervalue the power of personal interaction and relationships.

The little things we do in our life, the small courtesies, make a big difference, and connect us with each other.

When I was a kid, I had a great example of small acts of kindness and community building.

The Extra Chair

One year at Thanksgiving, Mom told me to set an extra place setting. We'd counted up all the relatives who would be coming, and I was curious as to who she was adding. By my count, we hadn't forgotten anyone and the place settings matched the numbers of who was coming.

"Oh, it's nice to have an extra setting, just in case," she said. "You never know who might come."

I was very curious, but she wouldn't answer my persistent questions.

Thanksgiving morning came and we were all put to work on preparations for the meal. My dad had to go into work for an hour, and not long after he left, the phone rang. It was my dad.

"That's fine," she said. "Of course. No problem. The table's already set and there's an extra chair."

She turned to us after she hung up the phone.

"We'll be having another guest for dinner," she said. She smiled then, and started humming a tune, as she turned back to the stove.

Sure enough, my dad arrived home with our mystery guest. She was a co-worker and had no other place to go for Thanksgiving. Her smile said it all, how grateful she was to be included.

Every year after that, we always set an extra place for Thanksgiving. One year there was a flood and some neighbors couldn't make it to their family dinner, so we set up another table and had another half dozen dinner guests.

One year, it was one of my friends in high school, needing a refuge from a tough time on the home front.

As always, my folks asked no questions, and passed no judgement. The unexpected guest was welcomed with open arms and the first serving of turkey.

My wife and I continued the tradition, welcoming friends, making sure there was a place at the table.

The first Thanksgiving we had our foster son, we made sure he felt welcome, as family gathered to enjoy the holiday.

And, as if on cue, the phone rang, and I heard myself saying, "Sure, of course there's room. We'd love to have him."

I made a special trip while the turkey was cooking and brought his brother home for the weekend. We made sure to make him feel welcome, a part of the family. He responded with a tear running down his cheek, as he sat down in the extra chair.

Years later, after my folks had passed away, and our kids were starting their own families and had moved away. It was just my wife and I who would be home for dinner.

"Let's set another place," my wife said. "You never know."

A few days before, she called first one and then another friend, friends who were single, and who, it turned out, would be alone for Thanksgiving.

"Of course, you're invited. We'll expect you at 1," I heard her say.

We set two extra plates that year, and the Thanksgiving celebration became even more special, as two lonely people found a warm home and bountiful table to share, and our friendship grew. Thanksgiving took on a new, richer meaning that year.

One of our traditions, just as we sit down for the meal, is for everyone to share their gratitudes with the rest of us. There is so much to be grateful in our lives, and we so often tend to skip over giving thanks on Thanksgiving. Instead, we slide into talk about a lot of other subjects, forgetting what the day is really about.

Thanksgiving truly is a day to celebrate our gratitudes and to give thanks. And, often what I am most grateful for is that extra chair, that extra place setting. I'm grateful for the company of someone who would otherwise be alone on the day we gather and give thanks for all that we have. And that list begins with being thankful for each other.

The "extra chair" theory works most everywhere. When in doubt, roll out the welcome mat and include someone in the event.

The conversations will become richer, and the spirits of gratitude and inclusiveness, and community, will enter the room.

When we broaden the meaning of "family", everyone benefits.

When a committee or a board, or a work group, takes on a problem, often people get stuck, and can't get some new ideas on the table. The conversation stagnates, reverting to old approaches, stale ideas, and the "tried and true" methodologies that really haven't solved the problem, but instead have "kicked the can down the road".

A new face, a fresh brain can spark new discussions and effective brainstorming.

"We've always done it this way" is replaced with excitement and new ideas.

So often we think we don't have the time for such conversations, or that some new thinking won't be productive.

Pull up that extra chair, invite that fresh perspective to the table. Maybe when you explain the problem or the relationship to someone new, something will spark, and a new synergy will emerge, and new ideas and approaches will stir everyone up. Solutions not imagined before will appear.

CONCLUSION

This book has taken us on a journey through a community, examining what makes us strong, what makes our lives meaningful, and gives us insight on who we are, where we've been, and where we are going.

"Times are hard," I often hear.

Difficult, challenging, confusing, depressing. Yes, and that has been true for every generation. We humans have persevered, and "powered through", taking what we have and making it better. We raise our kids, we strengthen institutions, we add something of our talents and brains to our communities. And, around the campfire, we tell our stories and express our values. We celebrate who we are, our individuality and our collective conscience, our community values. The form of the "community campfire" may change, but, fundamentally, we are hunters returning from the hunt to tell our stories and share our humanity, our collective "us".

Nationally, there is much lament and hand wringing over cultural affairs and loss of traditional, "wholesome" values. Yet, in the midst of all that noise and chatter, this community comes together and lives "in community".

I know the rest of the American nation also lives "in community", yet this sense of who we are and how we live is not newsworthy, and is often not celebrated in our culture with the same noise and drama that is normally saved for popular trends and fads, and the latest "headlines". These stories are often not told with the same sense of awe and excitement that we see in "popular" culture and national storytelling.

Today, these stories and our legacies need to be told, to be shared with others. In these story tellings, community is strengthened and passed on to new generations of movers and shakers, and storytellers.

Join me in this building community. It is a journey of opening hearts and letting deeply held and valued stories emerge. Listen with your own open heart, and be changed, and motivated to build your community.

With every conversation, with every act we perform, we are choosing if we are building community. Each one of us has a key role to play, and the ability to be a builder, a maker of a better world.

Rural America is in transition. There are many challenges, and often, the "tried and true" ways are not leading us to solutions and a better way of life. We are part of the world and the world is in need of new answers and new perspectives.

Each of us plays a part in this work.

The stories and opinions in this book are meant to help fill your own toolbox and to motivate you to take on this work and to make a difference.

Be a builder.

BUILDING COMMUNITY

QUOTES

"Men are free when they belong to a living, organic, believing community, active in fulfilling some unfulfilled, perhaps unrealized purpose. Not when they are escaping to some wild west. The most unfree souls go west, and shout of freedom." — D. H. Lawrence, *Studies in Classic American Literature*

"Creativity is just connecting things. When you ask creative people how they did something, they feel a little guilty because they didn't really do it, they just saw something. It seemed obvious to them after a while. That's because they were able to connect experiences they've had and synthesize new things."

--Steve Jobs

"Fire, ice, asteroids and pole shifts are bogeymen with which we distract ourselves from the real threat of our time. In an age when everyone invents his own truth, there is no community, only factions. Without community, there can be no consensus to resist the greedy, the envious, the power-mad narcissists who seize control and turn the institutions of civilization into a series of doom machines." — Dean Koontz, *Relentless*

"Shared values: vision, discipline, preparation, planning, and the binding power of aloha." --- Low, Sam, *Hawaiiki Rising: Hokule'a, Nainoa Thompson and the Hawaiian Renaissance,* p 325.

"To build community requires vigilant awareness of the work we must continually do to undermine all the socialization that leads us to believe in ways that perpetuate domination." —-Bell Hooks, *Teaching Community*

"One of the marvelous things about community is that it enables us to welcome and help people in a way we couldn't as individuals. When we pool our strength and share the work and responsibility, we can welcome many people, even those deep distress, and perhaps help them, find self-confidence and inner healing." —-Jean Vanier, *Community and Growth*

"Community is a word that alters in different contexts in almost chameleon-like fashion." —Sharon MacDonald, *A Companion to Museum Studies*

"Community is a group of individuals who have learned how to communicate honestly with each other, whose relationships go deeper than their masks of composure, and who have developed some significant commitment to 'rejoice together, mourn together", and to 'delight in each other, make others' condition our own'. " — M. Scott Peck, *The Different Drum*

"The essence of community, its heart and soul, is the non-monetary exchange of value; things we do and share because we care for others and for the good of the place." —— Dee Hock, *One From Many*

BIBLIOGRAPHY

Andrews, Andy. (2010) *The Butterfly Effect: How Your Life Matters.* Thomas Nelson: New York.

Bernstein, Nell. (2014) *Burning Down the House: The End of Juvenile Prison.* The New Press: New York

Booker, Cory. (2016) *United: Thoughts on Finding Common Ground and Advancing the Common Good.* Ballantine Books: New York

Brown, Brene'. (2017) *Braving the Wilderness: The Quest for True Belonging and the Courage to Stand Alone.* Random House: New York.

Cameron, Julia. (2015) *The Complete Artist's Way: Creativity as a Spiritual Practice, 25th Anniversary Edition.* Penguin Random House: New York.

Carter, Jimmy. (2014) *A Call to Action: Women, Religion, Violence and Power.* Simon and Schuster: New York.

Contreras, Alan, ed. (2019) *Edge of Awe: Experiences of the Malheur-Steens Country.*

Coplin, Amanda. (2012) *The Orchardist.* HarperPerennial: New York.

Davis, Adam, ed. (2012) *Taking Action: Readings for Civil Reflection.* The Great Books Foundation: Chicago.

Diamond, Jared. (2011) *Collapse: How Societies Choose to Fail or Succeed.* Penguin Group: New York

Eder, Michele Longo. (2008) *Salt in Our Blood: Memoir of a Fisherman's Wife.* Saltinourblood.com

Fallows, James and Fallows, Deborah (2019) *Our Towns: A 100,000 Mile Journey Into the Heart of America.* Vintage.

Gates, Melinda. (2019) *The Moment of Lift: How Empowering Women Changes the World.* Flatiron Books: New York

Giono, Jean. (1954) *The Man Who Planted Trees.* Chelsea Green Publishing: White River Junction, VT (2015)

Goodwin, Doris Kearns. (2018) *Leadership in Turbulent Times.* Simon and Schuster: New York

Greenwood, Daphne and Holt, Richard. (2015) *Local Economic Development in the 21ˢᵗ Century: Quality of Life and Sustainability.* Routledge: New York

Kahn, Si. (2010) *Creative Community Organizing: A Guide for Rabble Rousers, Activists, and Quiet Lovers of Justice.* Berrett-Koehler Publishers: San Francisco.

Kimmerer, Robin Wall. (2013) *Braiding Sweetgrass: Indigenous Wisdom, Scientific Knowledge and the Teaching of Plants.* Milkweed Editions: Minneapolis.

Kivel, Paul, *Boys Will Be Men: Raising Our Sons for Courage, Caring, and Community.*

Lankes, R. David. (2016) *Expect More: Demanding Better: Libraries for Today's Complex World. ExpectMoreLibrary.com*

Low, Sam. (2019) *Hawaiki Rising: Hokule'a, Nainoa Thompson and the Hawaiian Renaissance.* University of Hawaii Press: Honolulu.

McCullough, David (2018) *The Pioneers: The Heroic Story of the Settlers Who Brought the American Ideal West.* Simon and Schuster: New York.

Nouwen, Henri. (1992) *The Return of the Prodigal Son: A Story of Homecoming.* Doubleday: New York.

Obama, Barack. (2006) *The Audacity of Hope: Thoughts on Reclaiming the American Dream.* Crown Publishing Group: New York.

Parker, Priya. (2018) *The Art of Gathering.* Penguin Random House: New York.

Pollan, Michael. (2006) *The Omnivore's Dilemma: A Natural History of Four Meals.* Penguin Press: New York.

Powers, Richard Brian. (2011) *The Astoria Chinatown Conspiracy.* VirtualBookWorm.com

Treuer, David. (2019)*The Heartbeat of Wounded Knee: Native America from 1890 to the Present.* Riverhead Books: New York

Tutu, Desmond. (2015) *The Book of Forgiving: The Fourfold Path for Healing Ourselves and Our World.* HarperCollins: New York.

Van der Kolk, Bessel. (2015) *The Body Keeps the Score: Brain, Mind, and Body in the Healing of Trauma.* Penguin Books: New York.

Walker, Alice. (1982) *The Color Purple.* Houghlin Mifflin Harcourt: New York.

Walker, Peter. (2018) *Sagebrush Collaborations: How Harney County Defeated the Takeover of the Malheur Wildlife Refuge.* Oregon State University Press: Corvallis OR.

Weisman, Alan. (1998) *Gaviotas: A Village to Reinvent the World.* Chelsea Green Publishing: White River Junction, VT.

Winfrey, Oprah. (2019) *The Path Made Clear: Discovering Your Life's Direction and Purpose.* Flatiron Books: New York.

ABOUT THE AUTHOR

Neal C. Lemery is a retired lawyer and judge, who has lived on the northern Oregon coast throughout his life. A fourth-generation resident in his community, he volunteers with a variety of non-profits and committees, and has mentored youths throughout his career and retirement. A master gardener and guitar player in a local rock and country band, he also serves on the county library board. His three previous books celebrate community life and the transformation that people who engage with other people to improve lives at risk and community vitality. He and his wife, Karen Keltz, are often found in their garden, as well as writing and working to strengthen their community. His books can be found at Amazon.com.

Visit his website at http://neallemery.com .